Hope for Easter

Authentic

First published 2011 by Authentic Media Ltd
Presley Way, Crownhill, Milton Keynes, Bucks, MK8 OES
www.authenticmedia.co.uk

British Library Cataloguing in Publication Data
A catalogue record for this book is available from the British Library
ISBN-13: 978-1-86024-822-1

Printed in Great Britain by Bell & Bain Ltd., Glasgow

Contents

Introduction

Dear friends,

It's amazing to have you with us on this journey of HOPE! It's so exciting to think of the significant difference we will all be making to our communities as we step out in faith to tell people about God's incredible love.

Lent and Easter provide us with so many opportunities to tell the amazing news about what Jesus did for us on the cross two thousand years ago and how it can change lives today. We want to make the most of these opportunities, so this resource contains some great mission ideas that can be adapted and used for your village, town or city. You may want to join up with other churches in your area to work together in unity and make an even bigger impact on your community.

How to use this resource

You may want to join up with other churches in your area to work together in unity.

Whatever you choose to do, the most important thing is that we all do something! This resource is designed to give you all the materials you need to get your church engaged with the idea of mission around Easter. It would be fantastic if you could encourage the small groups in your church to use the Bible studies; these will help adults access the amazing story of Jesus' death and resurrection afresh and be envisioned again for mission. We'd love your youth leader to use the youth group sessions to help your young people engage with the Easter story and see how they can impact their community in Jesus' name.

As early as possible in the run-up to Easter, check out the ideas for mission, too, and see which you think would work in your community. Pick one or two to try – or more if you have the capacity! Some take very little resource, others need more planning. Some can be done by individuals; some would work best if the whole church is behind them. None of what we're suggesting is prescriptive. HOPE has always been about providing you with encouragement and resources but allowing you to decide what works best in your area.

There are also reflective articles in this resource where a number of Christians from different walks of life share what Easter means to them. We hope these will inspire you in your personal walk with God throughout this season.

HOPE beyond 2011!

In 2011 we're focusing on Easter, this is part of our bigger vision for HOPE to continue over the coming years. In 2012 we will be focusing on harvest; in 2013 we will look at how to put on fantastic summer events and make the most of the opportunities around Christmas. All of this will build towards 2014 where we're aiming to get thousands of churches across the nation to undertake a whole year of mission!

We want to do everything we can to support you, the local church, who are doing such an amazing job of bringing Jesus to those around you in word and deed. We'll be producing resources like this one to give you ideas to continue your mission work in your area. If you'd like to be kept informed of how to get hold of future publications, or you'd like to give us feedback on this one so we can continue to improve for the future, you can contact us at info@hopetogether.org.uk or through the website **www.hopetogether.org.uk**.

We'd also love to hear your stories of how everything you're doing is impacting your community, so please do visit our website to tell us what's been happening in your area.

God bless you as you seek to live out the Great Commission,

Roy Crowne

On behalf of the HOPE Leadership Team: Andy Hawthorne, Mike Pilavachi, Yemi Adedeji, Wendy Beech-Ward, Matt Bird, Ian Bunce, Gavin Calver, Steve Clifford, Rob Cotton, Colin Hardicre, Jane Holloway, Rachel Jordan, Wayne Malcolm, Kiera Phyo, Laurence Singlehurst and David Westlake.

We're aiming to get thousands of churches across the nation to undertake a whole year of mission in 2014.

We'd love to hear your stories of how everything you're doing is impacting your community.

Magnifying God's Love

Laurence Singlehurst

We all know that every missional endeavour must have prayer at its heart and as we look at HOPE for Easter we are convinced that prayer is the secret ingredient that makes everything work. It enlarges our heart so we are passionate, and it releases God's presence into the people and situations we hope to be involved in. But how does prayer work? If you're like me you may need continual inspiring and challenging; I know prayer is important, but sadly it is not my natural inclination.

> Every missional endeavour must have prayer at its heart.

So here is a fantastic illustration that has encouraged me for 20 years: When I was at school, some of us had 2-inch magnifying glasses. These magnifying glasses were not because we had poor eyesight, but they were for those hot sunny days when we could rush outside, find some of God's good creatures and focus the sunlight on them until they shrivelled or blew up. When we were bored with that we would find some unsuspecting person who we could lurk behind and focus the sunlight on their jumper or jacket and burn a nice little hole. Then, ultimately, the back of people's necks produced wonderful results as the sunlight burnt into their neck.

Now let us ask ourselves a question – what is going on here? Does the magnifying glass make the sun hotter? No, the magnifying glass simply focuses the sun into a specific place and that creates an impact. So when we pray does it make God love people more? No, but what it does is focus the love of God onto a particular place, person or event, and the focused love of God through prayer creates an impact. It burns away those things that hold people back; there is a greater sense of the presence and the love of God in those situations or activities.

Prayer is not just an adult activity, everyone can pray.

Personal

So how can we pray this Easter? Firstly, as an individual, think of yourself as that magnifying glass and focus on those people and situations where you want to see more of God's love and presence. Think of four or five people who need to know more of God's love, think of a dark situation that needs more of God's light, and pray yourself.

Small groups

I thought I understood small group praying until I met a friend who introduced me to Luke 10:2, which says, *'The harvest is plentiful, but the workers are few. Ask the Lord of the harvest, therefore, to send out workers into his harvest field.'* In other words, we often pray for events or for people (which is not bad) but Jesus' words talk about us as the labourers. My suggestion this Easter is that as you use this resource in your small groups, you take time at the end of your meeting to pray for two or three people in your group. Ask God to bless and use them as they seek to be an influence to their friends, to their situation and as they are involved in some of the Easter missional ideas. We are the labourers and we need God's presence and power to love our friends and to do the things God is saying to us.

Large groups

As we have this special Easter focus it would be great if we could join up with other churches within our community to pray together for God's blessing in our city, town or village. Let's pray that as we work together there would be a greater sense of God's presence and a greater understanding of who he is, that Jesus might be seen and understood and his message, his death and resurrection would touch people's hearts and minds.

Children and youth

Prayer is not just an adult activity, everyone can pray. Andy Kennedy from King's Kids has developed some great games that children can play which are fun and have prayer dynamics in them. You can find more details on **www.hopetogether.org.uk**. Let's also encourage teenagers to find creative ways to pray too; I was with one teenager who prayed as he drummed! Extremely noisy, but I'm sure God heard, so let's think of creative ways that we can all be involved in magnifying God's love and presence in our communities this Easter.

« What Easter Means to Me »

Stephen Timms, MP

Easter is the answer to despair. We spend a lot of time worrying about problems and struggling to solve them but, as we remember that Jesus rose from death, Easter puts our struggles in perspective. It's a crucial reminder that, one day, things which are obviously wrong today will be put right.

By highlighting that death is not the end, Easter confirms that we can afford to serve. Serving others may not appear to do us much good. There is a compelling argument for putting ourselves first instead. But Easter reminds us of the bigger picture: even death is not the end. Our long-term future is secure, so we have the freedom to do what is right. If I didn't believe in the resurrection, I would have little alternative but to pursue my own, narrow personal interests.

People often say you shouldn't mix faith and politics. I don't agree. In fact, my view is the opposite – that faith is a great starting point for politics because faith is the source of the values that we need to make politics work: responsibility, solidarity, persistence, compassion, truthfulness. And it's the events of Easter which, above all, make those values real for Christians. Easter proves that it's worth doing the right thing, rather than the expedient thing or the selfish thing. It's the reason Christians changed the political climate in Britain – 200 years ago to abolish the slave trade, or, in the past ten years, in *Jubilee 2000* and *Make Poverty History*, to increase Britain's international aid. It's the reason Christians are working in every community in the land – for example, supporting young people, helping people trapped in debt, or enabling people without jobs to find them. Above all, working to tell the good news that, through the events of Easter, we can now all become friends with God.

Agu Irukwu, Senior Pastor of Jesus House

Easter is a time when I feel incredibly weighed down by guilt, yet weightless and free. It's a time when I reflect on the life of Christ and resolve to be more like him. My gratitude for the gift of his life stirs up a burning desire to emulate the life he led on earth. He gave us clear guidelines on how he expects us to live and, if only for a period, I'm mindful of pleasing him, living like he did, mirroring his actions and words.

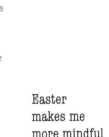

Easter helps me to appreciate the leadership of Christ. He was a leader of the people. He was no pen pusher; he got his hands dirty. He got involved in the lives of the people – he ate with them, drank with them, laughed with them and cried with them. He loved people deeply. He was no respecter of persons; he embraced everyone, from the greatest to the least. All were equal in his eyes. He was compassionate yet just. He provided for, healed and encouraged. He literally touched a man with leprosy and allowed a woman of the night to anoint his feet in public. He wasn't concerned with what the people thought about him, his primary concern was doing what was right. He was a man on a mission who did not relent until his mission was accomplished. He presented himself as he was and made no apologies for it. He wasn't a proud man, he was just a man who knew who he was and stood by what he believed in.

Easter makes me more mindful of Christ and his character; I can't escape thinking about what Jesus would do if he was living in these current times. He didn't twiddle his thumbs, he was a doer. He always got stuck in. As a 12-year-old, his distraught parents who had been searching for him, found him in the temple listening to and questioning the teachers. He asked questions, he challenged the thought processes of the people. He stood up for those who were defenceless.

> Easter makes me more mindful of Christ and his character.

The death of Christ bought me freedom to be salt and light. His resurrection is proof that he will return and I will have to account for how I have lived out his legacy. Impacting the world is not an option; it's a fundamental duty for me as a leader.

Tell us what Easter means to you at www.hopetogether. org.uk, on Twitter at www.twitter.com/hopetogether or on the HOPE Together Facebook page!

Rachel Gardner, Romance Academy

Falling in love can be very confusing. For starters you have to work out whether the feeling is love or something similar (like hunger, tiredness or boredom!). Then you have to work out how to let 'the one' know of your deep feelings without looking like a) a stalker b) an idiot c) both a stalker and an idiot! Once you have worked your way through both of these mine fields, you have to get on with the job of actually loving someone, day in and day out. And that really is the hardest part. Because although we have all been made for love, we have to learn the art of loving and being loved. We learn these love-lessons all the time. From our family, friends, culture, community, church. We are constantly analysing what is and what isn't real when it comes to love. We wade through the lies that tell us we are more loveable if we could just be better looking, a better daughter or son, a better Christian . . . then we'll be worth it.

You are worth loving.
You are worth dying for.
And someone did die for you.

When you realise this your life turns upside down and inside out. You start living and loving in outrageous ways. Just like the tomb Jesus burst out of, new life will rush out of you in a tsunami of love. And every Easter you will be reminded that the tomb is empty so that your heart need never be. Every Easter you will remember that Jesus gave it all up for you so that you can join him in giving every ounce of yourself to him, in his service.

You will fall in love all over again with the new life you have because of Jesus.

This Easter embrace the love. Live the love. Share the love.

> You will fall in love all over again with the new life you have because of Jesus.

Steve Clifford, Head of Evangelical Alliance

Things are never going to be the same again!

'What a waste of time, three years of my life.'

'I really thought he was "The One".'

'He made so much sense when we were with him. He was such fun to be with.'

'Remember the healings! Never seen anything like it – blind people seeing, lame walking, even the dead coming back to life!'

'Picnics which fed 5,000.'

'Walking on water, gallons of wine produced for a party.'

'They were so jealous. Couldn't fit him into their neat religious systems.'

'No one likes being called a hypocrite!'

'I never expected him to die. To die like a common criminal.'

'He failed us. All of us.'

I can empathise with the two disciples on their long walk home to Emmaus. I had a friend who caused me such a deep level of pain and disappointment, it made me ask questions like why didn't I see it coming? Could I have done more? We'd had Christmas together, been involved in evangelism together, planted a church together. He'd preached the gospel, prayed for the sick, people had come to Christ. He led a growing church. It was all going so well. Then it happened. Over the course of a few months he'd left his job, left his wife, given up living with his kids and closed his heart to God.

These two disciples on their way to Emmaus were mired in even deeper disappointment; they had hoped for so much and yet Jesus was obviously just another failed Messiah.

But then it happened, in a moment it all got turned around. It was the great reversal. This was Jesus after all. As he breaks bread and speaks, they suddenly recognise who he really is. Unbelievable! Death couldn't hold him . . . it was defeated forever. Sins could be forgiven; new life was available for all. Without a doubt things were never going to be the same again!

> Without a doubt things were never going to be the same again!

Ideas for Mission

Over the next few pages you'll find some great ideas for mission over Lent, Easter and beyond! The ideas focus on finding ways to build relationships with people in your community and are focused on evangelism through deed. This obviously doesn't mean we neglect the words element of telling people about Jesus! As you do acts of kindness for people they will probably ask you why you're doing them, so it's worth being prepared and thinking through how you would explain what God has done for you and what Easter is all about. Be careful to avoid jargon that might not make sense outside of a church context! It's also a great idea to have invitations to your Easter service (or to other church events) and booklets explaining Christianity ready to give out at events you run. (See the resources section of **www.hopetogether.org.uk**)

Be careful to avoid jargon that might not make sense outside of a church context!

We've suggested a timeline of activities that you might find useful but it's up to you to pick and choose what would work well, and when, in your community. You'll see that lots of the ideas can be adapted and run by individuals, small groups, churches and groups of churches across villages, towns and cities. So have a look through, see what inspires you and get planning as soon as possible to make sure this Easter your community knows the love of Jesus!

Lent
- Pancake party on Shrove Tuesday.
- Sacrificial giving.
- Collect for charity.*

Have a look through, see what inspires you and get planning.

In the run-up to Easter

- Art and photography exhibition and competition.
- Love your street.
- Schools work.
- Easter egg giveaway.*
- *Why I Love . . . film project.**

Easter Holidays

- Holiday clubs for kids.
- Football academy.*
- 24–7 prayer.*
- Spring clean.*

Good Friday

- Turn a 'walk of witness' into a 'wave of blessing'.
- Give away free hot cross buns in strategic places in your community e.g. railway station, shopping centre.
- Passion plays/choirs/children's musicals.

Easter Sunday

- Ideas to make the most of your Sunday service.

Easter Monday

- Fun Day with Easter themed activities.

After Easter

- Bless the servants in your community e.g. postmen, dustmen, police, doctors and nurses.

* In the **Mission Ideas for Young People** section on page 35.

Why not join with churches all around the world praying for hope in a world broken by poverty? Find out more about the Global Poverty Prayer Week at www.tearfund.org/onevoice

Pancake Party

Shrove Tuesday

(8 March 2011, 21 February 2012, 12 February 2013, 4 March 2014)

Great idea for individuals across towns, villages and cities!

Shrove Tuesday is traditionally a day of celebration, so it's a great day to kick off your HOPE Easter activities in your community! As the last day before Lent, Shrove Tuesday is a time to eat good things before the period of abstinence leading up to Easter begins. Pancakes became traditional as they contain eggs and fat which, historically, were not allowed during Lent. Whatever you're choosing to give up, pancakes are universally popular and 'Pancake Day' is a great excuse for a party!

A pancake party will probably work best in people's homes, so can be done as individuals or small groups inviting friends, family and neighbours round for a few pancakes. It doesn't need to cost lots of money – batter is cheap to make and you could provide wedges of lemon and bowls of sugar and ask your guests to bring their favourite sweet or savoury toppings.

NB: If you want to adapt this idea and provide pancakes for members of the public you may need to check Health & Safety guidelines.

> Shrove Tuesday is a time to eat good things before the period of abstinence leading up to Easter begins.

A pancake party will probably work best in people's homes, so can be done as individuals or small groups inviting friends, family and neighbours round for a few pancakes.

Consider

- Pancake races – a tradition that apparently began when a woman was making pancakes and heard the church bells ringing, calling her to worship. Realising she was late she ran out of the house with the frying pan still in her hand! Modern-day racers usually have to toss the pancake a certain number of times before they reach the finish line with their pancake intact.

- Pancake tossing – willing participants can challenge each other to see how many times they can toss a pancake in two minutes. The official world record stands at well over 400 times!

- Remember: pancake batter is easy to make and keeps well. Make a few batches the night before and keep them in the fridge so you have more time to enjoy with your guests on the night.

- With Lent starting the following day, Shrove Tuesday is a great time to get people to share what they would like to give up for Lent. You could ask members of your community if they would like to join you in raising money through Lent – keep reading to find out more!

Shrove Tuesday is a great time to get people to share what they would like to give up for Lent.

Sacrificial Giving

This idea can be used by individuals or by churches of any size. The more people who get involved, the bigger the impact!

In the run-up to Easter (Lent) we focus on what Jesus sacrificed for us. He gave everything, and going without one of our usual comforts for a short amount of time helps us to focus on his great and sacrificial love. But fasting is about more than just stopping doing something; it's about getting our hearts right with God and understanding his heart for the world.

We can use Lent as a time to bless our communities and show them God's sacrificial love.

What's the idea?

> Think of something you do on a regular basis, that costs you money and that you can give up for Lent.

Think of something you do on a regular basis, that costs you money and that you can give up for Lent. It could be something you give up completely (like chocolate) or something where you pick a cheaper alternative (like inviting a friend round for coffee instead of meeting at a coffee house). Keep track of the money you save each week and put it in a pot. If you do this as a whole church, have a pot there that people can put their money into.

Where does the money go?

What needs are there in your community that you could do something about? One church in Watford committed their money to their local hospital that was struggling to buy equipment for its children's ward. The hospital was stunned when the church promised over £5,000 – questioning whether an extra '0' had been added on by mistake! You could talk to local charities and projects about their needs, consider giving the money to a school that would benefit from some new equipment, or speak to the council about whether you could buy

Give up buying chocolate, downloading music or buying magazines for the duration of Lent.

apparatus for a park. Alternatively you could use the money to help those in poverty around the world. You could use the money raised to sponsor children through Compassion (www.compassionuk.org) or get involved with a national scheme called 'Lend Us Your Lent' run by Soul Action, a joint initiative between Soul Survivor and Tearfund. The money raised through Lend Us Your Lent will go to Tearfund and Soul Survivor partners in poor communities around the world (www.soulaction.org).

Ideas of what you can give up:

- Chose a cheaper brand in the supermarket.
- Make lunch at home instead of buying it at work.
- Rent a DVD instead of going to the cinema.
- Have a soft drink when you go to the pub instead of alcohol.
- Give up buying chocolate, downloading music or buying. magazines for the duration of Lent.

Make lunch at home instead of buying it at work.

If your church doesn't spend much money on luxuries then it might be that they'd like to donate some of their time instead. They could forgo a quiet Saturday morning or Sunday afternoon to clear an overgrown area, or offer a lunch break once a week to help a child in school learn to read. Finding out needs in the community that anyone could meet with a small amount of time gives people a great alternative if they are already living very simply financially.

Make a splash

When all the money has been received make a splash of handing it over to the recipients! Invite local press and members of the clergy to represent all the churches involved and present the money to the charity or organisation receiving it.

Art and Photography Competition

Great town- or city-wide idea!

The arts are a great way to engage with your community and competitions always draw a good response. The more local churches you involve, the bigger and better this idea will become!

What's the idea?

Run a competition to see who can produce the best image around an Easter theme e.g. 'hope' or 'new life'.

Launch the competition in schools, through community groups and consider advertising in local media.

Have three age ranges such as one for primary school children, one for secondary school and one for adults. Depending on your budget you could also have runners up in each category.

Budget some money for a cash prize (say around £250–£500 for each winner) which, in the adult category, could be donated to the charity of the winner's choice and for the young people could go towards art equipment at their school.

Create a community celebration by holding an exhibition of all the submitted works and having a prize-giving as part of the event.

Run a competition to see who can produce the best image around an Easter theme.

Consider

- Who your panel of judges will be. It's a great idea to include your mayor, a local art teacher, a local artist, church leaders, a local newspaper editor or a local radio presenter.

- Where you will have your exhibition. Your church building may be ideal or this could be a great chance to engage with members of the public elsewhere, for example at the local shopping centre or library. If you do this, just think about how you will make sure people know this is run by the churches!

- Prize alternatives. If you'd rather not give a cash prize you could also ask local businesses to provide prizes, or you could give prizes that will encourage the winner in their creative gift (e.g. art or photographic equipment).

- Media. Invite local press to take pictures of the prize-giving and to talk to one of the organisers. Be clear about why you've run the competition so they have a snappy 'sound-bite' that summarises your aims.

- Who will be at your exhibition. Churches who have held competitions like this have found images on the theme of 'hope' have often led to poignant conversations with members of the community so make sure you have some church members on hand during the evening just to talk to people.

Churches who have held competitions like this have found images on the theme of 'hope' have often led to poignant conversations with members of the community.

Love Your Street

Great idea for individuals, small groups and families!

Wouldn't it be amazing if each street in our community had someone who was committed to praying for it and making it a better place? As individuals, families, small groups, churches and Christians across villages, towns and cities we can make that a reality by each adopting a street to look after! It's a great way to start getting involved in your community and understanding its positive and negative aspects.

Anyone can put this into practice and you don't need any resources to make it happen!

> As God leads you, start to do things to bless that street and make it a better place.

▶ Pick a street you will commit to adopting. It could be where you live, where your small group meets, or a road you walk down regularly on your way to work, school or the shops.

▶ Pray for your street. You could do this every time you walk down it or set aside a specific time each week or month. Thank God for the good things that you see there. Pray about the bad things, asking him to bring change. Ask God what you can be doing to make a difference in that street.

▶ Take action. As God leads you, start to do things to bless that street and make it a better place. It could be as simple as picking up litter as you walk down it, or perhaps you will see a greater need in that area such as meeting someone who is homeless and in need of some food.

▶ Make friends and be hospitable! Purposefully and prayerfully look to start relationships with people who live or work on your chosen street. Start with one person or family and commit to praying for them and blessing them in any way you can. Open up your home and practise hospitality by inviting people round for dinner or a party.

This idea will be best driven by individuals but could be adopted around villages, towns and cities with someone co-ordinating which streets have been adopted so each one is covered. It would be fantastic to have regular prayer backing up the initiative, praying for situations arising in streets and keeping each Christian covered in prayer as they seek to bring God's kingdom to their street.

Schools Work

All of these ideas could be done by one church or you could work with others across your area to make them bigger and better!

Schools are right at the heart of the community and provide a great way to reach young people and their families. You don't need to be daunted if you've never worked with your local school, as Easter offers a multitude of reasons to get involved. Easter is part of the curriculum, so teachers are often very grateful for help, plus this could be a great chance to start conversations about other ways your church could be a blessing to them over the whole year.

A walk through the Easter story

Why not invite local school classes to visit your church in the run-up to Easter and re-enact the Easter story for them? St Polycarp's in Sheffield did just that with brilliant results! They visited schools first to teach the pupils some songs, chose 12 disciples and made palm leaves. Then they invited all the pupils into their church and walked them through the events using videos, a Passover meal, dramatic storytelling and song. The children and teachers loved it and we think it's an idea that could work brilliantly around the country!

Art and photography competition

See page 20 for more details on an art and photography competition which would work brilliantly in schools.

Taking lessons or assemblies

Many schools would welcome a visit from a Christian or a group from a local church to explain what Easter means to them and what happened over two thousand years ago. Why not approach your local school, start the process of getting to know them and see how you can help?

Further resources

There are lots of organisations who can help you deliver excellent schools work. Check out www.schoolswork.co.uk, www.yfc.co.uk, and www.scriptureunion. org.uk for more details. You can find out more about praying for schools at www.prayforschools.org.

> Why not invite local school classes to visit your church in the run up to Easter and re-enact the Easter story for them?

Holiday Clubs

The Easter holidays provide a perfect opportunity to bless families and connect with children in your community. Holiday clubs can be loads of fun, give parents a break and help children engage with church and God through fun activities like song, drama, craft, storytelling and games. There are loads of resources around that will give you plenty of ideas to make your holiday club a success with creative and interesting ideas. Try Scripture Union (www.scriptureunion.org.uk) whose holiday club materials for 2011 are based around a spy theme and will engage non-churched 5- to 11-year-olds with the story of Exodus. Or visit your local Christian bookshop in-store or online to browse a whole range of holiday club materials.

You could consider launching an in-school lunchtime club on the back of this to continue engaging with young people all year round.

> The Easter holidays provide a perfect opportunity to bless families and connect with children in your community.

Holiday clubs can be loads of fun, give parents a break and help children engage with church and God through fun activities.

Turn a Walk of Witness into a Wave of Blessing

For hundreds of years Christians have joined together to take part in a walk on Good Friday to remember Jesus' journey from his trial to the place of his crucifixion. Others have been involved in a parade on Easter Sunday to witness to Jesus' resurrection.

If these are key traditions in your church calendar, why not use them as another opportunity to show God's love to your community? Consider how your walk could be a blessing to others and how you could invite them to join in the celebration of Easter.

You could:

▶ Hand out goodies as you walk along, with invitations to your Easter Sunday service e.g. helium balloons, chocolates or hot cross buns.

▶ Take time to stop and chat to those around.

▶ End the walk with an open-air service of praise and thanksgiving.

▶ Or you could finish the walk by stopping somewhere central and offering to pray for local people who would like to be healed. 'Healing on the streets' started at a church in Northern Ireland and is being replicated around the UK, seeing many healed and come to faith after they have been prayed for. See the HOPE website **www.hopetogether.org.uk** for more details of this initiative.

> Hand out goodies as you walk along, with invitations to your Easter Sunday service.

Further resources

CPO offer lots of great resources you could use. Find out more at www.cpo-online.org.uk.

Creativity at Easter

Easter provides lots of opportunities to use the creative arts and this is a great way to work with other churches across your village, town or city to put on the best show you can! Using drama and music is a great way to engage a wide audience and to make sure the message of Easter is heard in your community.

Passion plays

You could work with other churches in your area to put on a simple performance of a Passion play.

Passion plays have been part of the church tradition for many years, telling the story of Jesus' trial, death and resurrection. Often churches perform their play in the open air, attracting passing crowds, and sometimes moving to different locations for changing scenes. Don't forget to pool resources with other churches to make sure you have a big enough team to take care of the scripting, acting, publicity, costumes and sets! If you're going to be doing the play outside, speak to your local council first.

Think about how to make the play relevant to your area. You might want to keep very strictly to the words and actions shown in the Bible or you could give the play a more contemporary feel using popular music and modern-day language.

Further resources

The Mystery and the Passion by Richard Hasnip, book £7.99, www.saltminetrust.org.uk.

Children's musicals

A great way to engage children is to put on a children's musical around Easter either through local schools or churches. You could work with other churches in your area to put on a simple performance of a Passion play – a perfect excuse for a visitor service! Composer Sheila Wilson has written three Easter musicals to suit different age groups (4–8, 5–11 and teenagers). Each musical is around 15–25 minutes long and captures the hopes, the fears and, finally, the joy of the resurrection, bringing Scripture alive powerfully through children's voices. All the resources you need (including backing music if you're short on musicians) can be found at www.redheadmusic.co.uk.

'Children of Hope' – free resources!

'Children of Hope' is a song for 4–12-year-olds, written especially for HOPE by children's composer Sheila Wilson. With optional two-part harmonies, kazoos and hand-jives, its positive message makes a fun contribution to any event and is a great way to involve children and parents from the community! Download a live recording, a word sheet, a vocal manuscript and a chord sheet for free at **www.hopetogether.org.uk**.

Easter choirs – great idea for all ages!

Choirs are becoming increasingly popular, with many using modern and popular music and attracting all ages. This is a great opportunity for outreach. Gather a group of enthusiastic singers from both the church and the surrounding community and begin rehearsals. It could just be for the fun of singing together or you could put on a performance over the Easter weekend, perhaps charging a small entrance fee with all proceeds going to a local charity. Encourage the choir to invite all their friends and family to support them!

Choirs are becoming increasingly popular, with many using modern and popular music and attracting all ages.

Easter provides lots of opportunities to use the creative arts and this is a great way to work with other churches.

Making the Most of Your Easter Sunday Service

Lots of people come to church at Easter who wouldn't normally be there and hopefully with all the outreach you've been doing over Lent that number will increase this year! This means your Easter Sunday service is a fantastic opportunity to bring to life the truth about Jesus' death and resurrection.

Dramatic storytelling

This could be a great time for one or two of your church members to say what Easter means to them.

- Bring the story of Easter to life by having different members of the congregation learn sections of Scripture and then deliver them dramatically as part of the service.

- You could use video clips for some sections (Mark's gospel reads a little like headline news so you could record someone reporting the events as news).

- You could share breakfast when you get to the reading in John 21 where Jesus gives his disciples fish for breakfast.

- Think about symbolic gestures like flinging open the church doors when you proclaim the words of the Great Commission.

- You could have children perform a short Passion musical (see page 26 for more details).

You could take your service out onto the streets by doing an 'Emmaus walk', going from one place to another and, as you go, retelling the story of Jesus meeting the disciples on the road.

This could be a great time for one or two of your church members to say what Easter means to them (see page 94 for more details).

Don't forget!

- Make sure you have plenty of 'Welcome packs' to give to visitors which explain what your church is about and what else you do outside of a Sunday service. You might like to give them a gift, too, such as a small Easter egg as well as a Gospel to take home and read.
- After the service invite people to stay and share hot cross buns with you as part of the celebrations.
- Invite visitors to an upcoming social event that will take place a week or two after the service to help cement connections with newcomers.

Further resources

Pam Pott offers workshops to those who would like help, and advice on how to memorise Scripture and read it aloud dramatically.
Contact pam.pott@gmail.com.

Make sure you have plenty of 'Welcome packs' to give to visitors which explain what your church is about and what else you do outside of a Sunday service.

Fun Day

A free fun day is a great way to get the community together and bless people! Since HOPE began, churches around the UK have been running loads of brilliant days and have seen them make a huge impression. You could join with other churches in your area to make the biggest impact and see how much fun you can have!

The Easter Bank Holiday weekend can be a great time to have a fun day and you can do loads of Easter-themed activities like:

- Free hot cross buns or Easter eggs.
- Egg rolling race.
- Easter egg hunt for children.
- Passion play (see page 26 for more details).
- Have a large screen playing an Easter film.
- Free shoe cleaning (linking to Jesus washing the disciples' feet).
- Kids' craft tables making Easter cards and hats.
- Kids' Easter bonnet competition.

There are also loads of other great ideas to make your Easter fun day a blessing to the community:

- A bouncy castle.
- Market stalls.
- A free hog roast and refreshments.
- Face painting for kids.
- Having a prayer space where there's an opportunity for people to take some time for reflection or to be prayed for.
- Using a large screen to play a film related to HOPE. You could even film local people asking them about their hopes for the community and show that.
- Choir performances (see page 27 for more details).
- Pottery painting.
- Games like 'hook a duck' and 'bash the rat'.
- Puppet shows.

- A penalty shoot-out. You could invite local schools to take part and have a prize ready for the winners.
- Use the talents available in your church by getting any musicians or dancers to do workshops with young people.

> A great way to attract a teenage crowd is to have a stage and invite them to perform as bands or individuals. You could do auditions ahead of time or run an open-mic slot that people sign up for on the day. How about making it a competition and inviting a local celebrity to be one of the judges? The competition could take place during the afternoon or could be an event that takes place in the evening.

Consider

- Speaking to the local council about health and safety regulations.
- Consider what venue options you have if the weather is bad.
- Advertising your event in advance. Give your congregation flyers to hand to their friends, do a door-to-door drop, speak to local schools and advertise through local community groups that work with young families.
- Call your local newspaper and radio station to tell them about the day, they may cover the story in advance and on the day.
- Having HOPE branding at the event with your church details and website e.g. on T-shirts for your team and on banners around the venue.
- Don't forget to hand out flyers telling people about your Easter services and upcoming church events!

Call your local newspaper and radio station to tell them about the day.

Further resources

There are lots of organisations that could help you put on an amazing fun day by providing everything from a live band, to a barbecue, to a trained team to make everything happen! Check out details on the following websites:

Re:Act www.urbansaints.org

Youth For Christ www.yfc.co.uk (look in the 'Teams' section)

On the Move (www.onthemove.org.uk) can organise a large-scale barbecue and everything you need to go with it!

Serving the Servants

On the Thursday before Easter, also known as Maundy or Holy Thursday, we remember how Jesus washed the feet of disciples, demonstrating the kind of service and love we're to display to the world. This provides us with a great opportunity to go out in our communities and show them the servant-hearted love of Jesus.

Often these servants work long hours, and don't always receive much appreciation.

There are so many people who work day in, day out to serve our communities. We couldn't function without postmen, refuse collectors, lollipop ladies/men, nurses, youth workers, bus drivers, doctors, teachers, police officers, local council workers, and many more! Often these servants work long hours, and don't always receive much appreciation. Wouldn't it be amazing if we could show these servants that their work is noticed and that we're grateful for all they do?

The idea is simple: find a modern-day equivalent of washing someone's feet and head out as an individual, family, small group or church and say thank you! You could give out small gifts like flowers or chocolates and accompany them with a card that says the receiver is really appreciated for all they do in your area. You could also say that you're praying for them and give them a way to contact you with any prayer requests (such as an email address). The idea isn't to do a hard-sell, but to find simple ways to say thank you, to bless people and to demonstrate that we serve a loving and generous God.

Say thank you and demonstrate that we serve a loving and generous God.

More Ideas

Passover/Easter meal

Meals are a great way to create an informal atmosphere and encourage community, and a Passover feast gives an opportunity for everyone to see what Jesus' Last Supper would have been like. For ideas and recipes see the Scripture Union resource *Easter Cracked*. Invite friends, colleagues and neighbours, and take some time during the evening to share something about the message of Easter. You could also give your guests goody bags to take home with an Easter card, a booklet about what Easter is, and perhaps a gift as well.

For young people you could even have a different take on the Last Supper by putting on a Murder Mystery evening!

Hot cross buns

Find significant places in your community where there will be good passing traffic and hand out hot cross buns as a small celebration of Easter. This works well at places like train stations and shopping centres.

Easter eggs

Easter eggs are always popular too. How about getting your church members to donate eggs then giving them to social services or the local hospital to give to children who wouldn't normally receive gifts at Easter?

Films

Use great films like *The Passion of The Christ* to share the Easter story. You could put on a film night at your church, in your home or buy copies of the DVDs to give away.

Narnia

St Mary's church in Luton used the popular C.S. Lewis story *The Lion, the Witch and the Wardrobe* to attract attention to their church. They put a wardrobe in their doorway so that people literally entered through it, and hung coats there to make it authentic. It attracted lots of people who were walking past to come and see what was going on! You could then theme your talk around elements of the story and/or show the clips where Aslan is slain/resurrected representing what happened to Jesus.

> Hand out hot cross buns as a small celebration of Easter.

Food packages

If you know someone in your street who is struggling financially or going through a hard time, you could put together a food parcel to bless them over Easter.

Clean-up

Do you have a run-down estate near you? Get a team from your church together and organise a day or two of cleaning! Work out in advance what would be most beneficial to the community and think about things that are the modern-day equivalent of washing someone's feet. For example, wouldn't people start to ask questions if you hired a jet hose to clean out their outdoor bins for them?

You've probably got lots of other ideas too! Why not share them with others on the HOPE website? You'll also find further mission ideas from us there as well!
www.hopetogether.org.uk

General resources

J. John *Easter Sonrise* is a short booklet explaining the truth and significance of Easter. Available from www.philotrust.com/shop for £1 per copy (bulk order discounts apply).

Biblefresh are running a project called *You've Got the Time* to help people engage with the Bible more deeply by listening to the New Testament over 40 days. To find out more call 01793 418222. They are also offering five short Bible reflections on Easter, available to download from www.grow-with-the-bible.org.uk.

Square Mile is an Evangelical Alliance initiative which aims to catalyse and equip Christians to take a truly integrated approach to mission. For information go to www.eauk.org/squaremile.

Discovery is a practical course from Tearfund designed to help your church become a transforming influence within your local community. For information go to www.communitymission.org.uk.

Just People Course is a six-week course developed by Community Mission, a partnership between Livability and Tearfund, equipping churches to respond to local and global poverty. For more information go to www.communitymission.org.uk.

Mission Ideas for Young People

In addition to the other ideas in this resource, you might like to consider these for your youth group.

Easter Football Academy

Sport is great for uniting communities and the Easter holiday provides a great opportunity to encourage young players to build their skills, self-esteem and to have some fun. So why not put on a football academy for one week over the Easter holidays? The sessions could be just a morning or afternoon and run Monday to Friday.

Why not put on a football academy for one week over the Easter holidays?

Consider

- Hiring an FA qualified coach or asking a football enthusiast you know to take the sessions.

- Involving members of your team who will make good mentors and role models to the young people who come along.

- What you will charge. Sometimes people respond better when there is a small charge as they believe the course will be more valuable than if it's offered for free. You may, however, want to offer some free places to families who can't afford the cost.

- Have a short pep talk or teaching session as part of each day where you tie in an element of the story of Easter with football. For example, you could talk about the sacrifice Jesus made and the sacrifices needed in sport. You could also talk about issues that are particularly affecting young people in your area like knife crime or bullying.

- Allow opportunities for relationships to be built, perhaps over a light lunch.

- On the last day, make time to give an award or certificate to each person that takes part. This is great for building self-esteem and also gives an opportunity to invite parents along so you can engage with them too.

Collect for Charity

A practical way to help a charity while also getting your young people thinking about physical and spiritual 'junk' in their lives.

What's the idea?

At the start of Lent ask your young people to go through their wardrobes and put anything they haven't worn or used for six months in a bag. At Easter ask them to bring in anything in this bag which they still haven't worn or used. Together, take all the contents of these bags to a local charity shop.

Encourage the young people to be really honest about how much they can afford to give away. Challenge them not to go too easy on themselves. On the other hand, try to make sure they're not being over-zealous and giving away a great deal, or expensive items, unnecessarily. It might be wise to let parents know what you're doing so they can help with this.

Egg Giveaway

> Encourage the young people to be really honest on how much they can afford to give away.

A great idea for the last day of the school term; using chocolate to share the true message of Easter!

What's the idea?

Challenge your young people to give out a small Easter egg to each of their friends/classmates and use it to explain the importance of new life. It has been known for some youth groups to lead assemblies in their schools explaining this, with the local church sponsoring giving a chocolate egg to every student. This is a creative way of sharing the Easter story and challenging the young people to share their faith.

Consider

- How will you get enough eggs? Perhaps contacting a confectionery company to discuss what you're doing could yield a cheap bulk order. It would definitely be worth getting your church's backing for this project and asking for their financial support.

- Who will do the talking? Make sure your young people are confident explaining the message of new life behind Easter. If the project involves any public speaking, make sure those doing the talking are comfortable with this role.

24–7 Prayer

This can really help to inspire your young people in their prayer lives, and to develop their heart for their community. It can also be surprisingly effective at drawing in your young people's friends or those on the fringes of the group.

What's the idea?

Set aside a particular room for prayer in your church, community centre, or even school. Fill the room with materials to inspire people to pray and to enable them to pray creatively. It also helps to cover the walls with paper (to draw on) and to use cushions and throws to make the room more comfortable. You could even set up curtains to form a 'Holy of Holies'. Encourage your young people to sign up for hour-long slots, and in this way try to cover every hour of a week or weekend with prayer. Involve adults in the church, too, and encourage the young people to bring their friends to pray.

Consider

- Who will be involved? Your young people are likely to provide the impetus for this kind of season of prayer, but the more people you can get behind the idea, the better. So who else from your church and from other churches in your area can you get on board? And how can you encourage young people from your church to get their friends involved?

- Logistics. There is work to be done in setting up the room, but also in arranging how people will sign up, how people will access the room, separate rooms to sleep in and the all-important tea and coffee facilities.

- Corporate prayer. A few times of group prayer in the room can add renewed energy. Try to start and finish the season of prayer with a time of corporate prayer and worship.

- Child protection. Ensure that nobody under 18 is ever left in the building alone or with just one adult. Also provide two separate rooms which boys and girls can sleep in, if they need to.

> This can really help to inspire your young people in their prayer lives, and to develop their heart for their community.

Further resources

For more inspiration, creative ideas and logistical tips, see www.24-7prayer.com.

For resources on running 24–7 Prayer rooms in schools go to www.prayerspaceinschools.com/home.

One Voice: Join 24–7 Prayer, Tearfund and hundreds of churches and youth groups around the world for a week of prayer. For more information go to www.tearfund.org/youth.

Who else from your church and from other churches in your area can you get on board? And how can you encourage young people from your church to get their friends involved?

Spring Clean

What's the idea?

Get your young people together for a day cleaning up their town. Provide them with all the equipment they're likely to need, divide them into teams, and set about clearing up rubbish, cleaning graffiti, digging gardens, painting garages and whatever else your community needs.

This project will be much more effective if you spend some time beforehand working out what the real needs of your community are. For example, talk to your local council or residents' association. Then target two or three particular areas of town and give them a deep clean. Or you could pick a particular street, speak to residents and ask them what they would like your team to do.

If managed well, this project will make a lasting difference to your area and be a brilliant example of how the church can serve communities. It can also inspire your young people to put their faith into action, and develop group dynamics.

Consider

- Equipment. Make sure your group have all the tools they need for the tasks in hand. You may need to enlist the help of the wider church in providing tools or the funds to buy equipment.

- Health and safety. Make sure anything you plan is properly risk-assessed. And again, child protection must be a consideration, so make sure you have enough adults helping to lead the project.

- Although the young people won't be getting paid for their work, it is important to make sure that they do the best job possible, so leader monitoring on the day is essential.

- Local Media. This is a great chance to show others that not all young people fit the media stereotype, so invite local press along to see the amazing work that the young people are doing.

Invite local press along to see the amazing work that the young people are doing.

Why I Love . . . Film Project

Using film for capturing moments and thoughts has become a common part of most young people's lives, so why not harness that to produce a piece of history about what your young people think about the place in which they live?

What's the idea?

▶ Challenge young people to film a 2–3-minute video showing or explaining the things that they love about their area and community.

▶ When the videos are collected, the best ones will be compiled to make a film entitled *Why I Love [insert town name]*.

▶ Launch the project in schools and youth clubs around the town, offering a prize and certificate for all the films included in the final film.

▶ Create a website or YouTube channel where the videos can be uploaded and viewed by others.

▶ Arrange a premiere for the film, invite the young people and their families plus local dignitaries and possibly a celebrity to give out prizes.

Produce a piece of history about what your young people think about the place in which they live.

Consider

• Parental consent. You will need written consent for the young people to feature in the final film. You can achieve this with a simple form.

• What your prizes will be. You will need to give them some incentive, but you may have a lot of people involved in the short film, so cost could be an issue. You could get a local business to support the project to help cover costs.

- Who will edit the final film. You will need someone with very good editing skills to make sure that the finished article is up to scratch. The young people will be expecting it to look professional.

- Where you will have your premiere. You need a location that you can make look nice but also project the film, like a cinema. You need to think about who you would like to attend, when considering the venue.

- Media Coverage. If you release some clips to local TV and radio you can give the project a wider final viewership.

- How the film will be made available. You must decide how the final film will be viewed or purchased (either though a website or sale at the event). You could send copies to local schools and groups that were involved.

> If you release some clips to local TV and radio you can give the project a wider final viewership.

Using film for capturing moments and thoughts has become a common part of most young people's lives.

« *What Easter Means to Me* »

Rt Hon. Caroline Spelman MP

Easter is a special time for me as I was originally confirmed on Palm Sunday and the dynamic of Holy Week reminds me of that important decision I made in adult life to confirm the faith in which I was raised as a child. I always remember Good Friday being a day of reflection in the village in which I grew up. The parish church in which my father was an usher was stripped of its ornaments and the mood of the 3 p.m. service was sombre. When I went to work in France, I was astonished that Good Friday is a regular working day, which demonstrates the power of secularism. It felt all wrong as it should be a day of remembering everything that Jesus did for us.

The contrast between Good Friday and Easter Day couldn't be stronger with the church transformed by the joy of celebrating Jesus' resurrection. The sombre mood is gone and instead churches are filled with spring flowers reminding us of life bursting forth from the grave. The whole dynamic is a microcosm of our individual journey from a certain death without faith to eternal life with it.

Ian Bunce, Head of Mission, Baptist Union

The ministry of Jesus begins with the phrase 'Blessed are the peacemakers' and ends with the ultimate act of peacemaking. From the clearing of the temple to the intimate meal with friends in an upper room, Jesus actively worked to bring peace to a troubled world. The ultimate sacrifice of God made flesh hanging on a cross was about bringing peace into a confusing world.

After Jesus' death, trouble filled the hearts of many. 'What has happened, and what do we do now?' they asked. Yet in the post-resurrection appearances of Jesus we hear him say time and time again, 'Peace be with you.'

It was in John 21 we saw this lived out in an acute way. Peter, the loud-mouthed disciple (who I can relate to very much), had failed Jesus at his darkest hour and was a broken man. We read how when he denied Jesus before the cock crowing, he ran out and wept bitterly; he knew nothing but torment and trouble. To escape he had gone back to his old occupation of fishing, but even that was not successful. Jesus, the very man who Peter had failed, met him at a beach breakfast barbecue. Imagine the scene: you had let this guy down and messed up, yet here you are together. What is he going to do or say? There is no argument or fight; there is a restoration, a giving and receiving of peace, a place of renewed friendship and new trust for Peter. A place of commissioning and forgiveness, a place of making peace again with Jesus. Easter is a holy time, yes, a time of remembering and certainly a time of celebration. But it can also be a time when we meet with God and make peace with him. From that place we go on to be peacemakers in the world in which we live.

Where will you meet with Christ this Easter and receive restoration and purpose?

> The ultimate sacrifice of God made flesh was about bringing peace into a confusing world.

Rt Revd Paul Bayes, Bishop of Hertford

Bishop Tom Wright was in a taxi chatting to the driver, when the (Christian) driver said, 'The way I look at it is this: if God raised Jesus Christ from the dead, all the rest is basically rock 'n' roll.'

That's a pretty biblical taxi driver (check out 1 Corinthians 15:14: 'if Christ has NOT been raised, our preaching is useless and so is your faith').

HOPE is an opportunity to make a difference, as Christians work together to do more in word and deed. Without the resurrection of Jesus Christ, though, HOPE is just some useful social work together with a few useless words. Maybe that makes a bit of a difference – but we hope for more than that. Because of the resurrection, for the lives of thousands of people, HOPE can make *all* the difference, as they accept the truth of the risen Christ and come to know him themselves. All the rest is basically rock 'n' roll.

It's not always easy to be a Christian disciple. Our own sin, the brokenness of the church, the fallenness of the world – it can make the life of faith seem more like dark heavy metal than joyous rock 'n' roll. At moments like that we need to remember that ours is a faith based on miracles – and on this miracle most of all, that all darkness has been dispelled by the mystery of God's power in the life of the Lord Jesus. That everything Jesus said and did was vindicated by his Father's word of life that shattered death.

What does Easter mean to me? It means a difference. The same difference it meant to that taxi driver, and Bishop Tom, and St Paul, and you too – that is, *all* the difference.

If God raised Jesus Christ from the dead, all the rest is basically rock 'n' roll.

John Glass, General Superintendent, Elim Pentecostal Churches

The Easter story centres around the cross but, for a moment, I suggest that we might direct our focus on two characters nestled in the crowd. Though they were very different in background they had one common denominator that cemented them together and it was this: though they had come to faith in Jesus, and believed that he was the Messiah, each had failed to make a stand and 'come out' as believers.

Joseph of Arimathea was a secret disciple because he was afraid of the Jews. Nicodemus was similarly silent about what he now knew to be true; the Scriptures take the trouble to advise us that he ventured to speak to the Lord 'under the cover of darkness'. Even after learning how to be born again he kept the revelation 'in the dark' knowing that it might spell the end of his position as a religious leader.

As they simultaneously witnessed Jesus dying in open shame on the cross, we can imagine their eyes meeting as they resolved that, having failed to identify with Jesus when he was alive, they would not fail to do so in his death. Choosing the most public of all platforms for an act of courage that spontaneously sprang to life, John 19:38 records that Joseph of Arimathea asked Pilate for the body of Jesus. With Pilate's permission, he came and took the body away. He was accompanied by Nicodemus, the man who earlier had visited Jesus at night. Theirs was a resurrection that took place before Jesus even entered the tomb – courage that had died had come alive again.

Theirs was a resurrection that took place before Jesus even entered the tomb.

Tell us what Easter means to you at www.hopetogether.org.uk, on Twitter at www.twitter.com/hopetogether or on the HOPE Together Facebook page!

Paul Harvey, Managing Partner, Morrisons Solicitors LLP

For me, the most important question in the whole of history is, 'Did Jesus Christ rise from the dead?' The resurrection is absolutely vital to the Christian faith for without it there is no good news and the followers of Jesus are either deceived or deluded. (As the apostle Paul said, 'If Christ has not been raised, your faith is futile,' 1 Corinthians 15:17). As a lawyer, one of my essential tasks is to consider evidence and establish the facts. The fact that Jesus Christ is a historical figure is beyond dispute and is established by both Christian and non-Christian writers and historians. It is also a historical fact that he was crucified and that a short time later his followers claimed that he had risen from the dead.

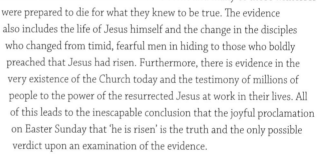

As a young lawyer I studied the evidence for the resurrection. There were eye witnesses whose testimonies were consistent and many of those witnesses were prepared to die for what they knew to be true. The evidence also includes the life of Jesus himself and the change in the disciples who changed from timid, fearful men in hiding to those who boldly preached that Jesus had risen. Furthermore, there is evidence in the very existence of the Church today and the testimony of millions of people to the power of the resurrected Jesus at work in their lives. All of this leads to the inescapable conclusion that the joyful proclamation on Easter Sunday that 'he is risen' is the truth and the only possible verdict upon an examination of the evidence.

Because 'he is risen', my destiny is secure and my everyday life has purpose. It is the risen Christ that I serve in my workplace and it is his presence and power that enables me and drives me to fulfil his calling there. The resurrection, therefore, is not just a historical fact but an everyday reality that has changed my life.

Because 'he is risen', my destiny is secure and my everyday life has purpose.

Lend Us Your Lent!
Materials for Youth Groups

Notes to youth leaders

The following pages contain materials for youth leaders to help navigate young people through Lent (the run-up to Easter) and Easter itself. There are four sessions, each with about an hour's worth of ideas that can be used on a Sunday or at a mid-week gathering.

Each session has points for discussion, ideas for prayer, games and action points; and you can pick and choose which elements you think will work well with the individuals in your group and with the time and resources you have. For example, if your youth are enthusiastic when it comes to group discussions you will need to allow extra time for these elements and cut out something else so the session doesn't overrun.

Lend Us Your Lent starts with giving something up, but is about so much more than that.

Items needed

For the sessions it would be useful to have small pieces of paper and pens available for the group to write individually, as well as large pieces of paper and marker pens to gather ideas from the group. For some elements of the sessions there will be additional items needed (such as a way to video your group in Session 1 and materials like blindfolds for games in Session 2), so please do check through the plan in plenty of time and see what you'll need.

About the materials

These materials have been provided by Soul Action (www.soulaction.org) which is a joint initiative between Soul Survivor and Tearfund that exists to encourage young people to live out God's mission in their everyday lives. You can find out more about Soul Action, get involved in Soul Action campaigns, tell your stories, watch videos and find lots of resources including a *Lend Us Your Lent* video at www.soulaction.org. You can also contact the Soul Action team by emailing info@soulaction.org to get copies of the *Lend Us Your Lent* leaflet.

Lend Us Your Lent is an idea being run by Soul Action that starts with giving something up, but is about so much more than that. It's not about ticking the Lent box and staying unchanged by Easter; it's about connecting with God, to understand his heart for those living in poverty and to find ways to get into action to serve others.

To give you a quick overview this is how the sessions look:

1. Give Something Up

This session explores why we fast (give things up) at Lent, what kinds of things we might want to give up and what benefit fasting can have for us. (NB: You might want to run this the week before Lent starts!)

2. Give Something Back

Sacrificing things to focus on God begins to change our hearts. We'll be focusing on the words of Isaiah 58 to look at how God wants us to live and get some ideas of how we can give to others.

3. Connect With God

Jesus did something amazing for us at Easter that means we can have a relationship with God! Through the story of the thief next to Jesus on the cross we'll look at how that relationship is open to others and how we can help be a part of connecting them to God.

4. Bless Others

Jesus left us a job to do. He came to serve the last, the least and the lost, and he asks us to do the same. How can our words and deeds impact those around us?

Jesus did something amazing for us at Easter.

Lend Us Your Lent is about connecting with God, to understand his heart for those living in poverty and to find ways to get into action to serve others.

Session 1: Give Something Up

When I was a young man, I wanted to change the world. I found it was difficult to change the world, so I tried to change my nation. When I found I couldn't change the nation, I began to focus on my town. I couldn't change the town and as an older man, I tried to change my family. Now, as an old man, I realise the only thing I can change is myself, and suddenly I realise that if long ago I had changed myself, I could have made an impact on my family. My family and I could have made an impact on our town. Their impact could have changed the nation and I could indeed have changed the world.

(Unknown)

What's it all about?

This session is about why we fast during Lent, how it can change us and help us connect to God, and begins to get us thinking about how our fasting could be of benefit to others.

Icebreaker: Easter Pictionary (5–10 minutes)

Write different catchphrases or words associated with Easter on small pieces of paper. Divide the group into two teams and have a person from each ready to draw on a large piece of paper in front of their team. Give each team two or three minutes to draw and guess as many words as they can.

Has anyone given up anything for Lent before? If so, what did they give up and why?

Think (5 minutes)

Before Jesus started his ministry he spent 40 days in the desert fasting (see Matthew 4:2) and focusing on God. In recognition of this and Jesus' sacrifice for us on the cross, Lent is a great time to fast and prepare ourselves for the celebration of Easter.

Has anyone given up anything for Lent before? If so, what did they give up and why?

God's people have fasted throughout history. In the Bible we read about the likes of Moses, David, Elijah, Esther, Daniel, Paul and of course Jesus, all fasting. Christians throughout Church history have also fasted such as Martin Luther, John Calvin, John Knox and Jonathan Edwards. John Wesley required every minister in the Methodist Church to fast for two days every single week!

But why fast?

Fasting helps us focus on God and demonstrates that he is more important to us than absolutely anything else in our lives. By giving things up we can find a new freedom and create space to connect with God. As we connect with God we begin to see the world through his eyes. Our faith then becomes less about just meeting our needs and more about meeting the needs of others.

Activity (15 minutes)

Fasting would normally require going without food and any form of liquid other than water. Lent is 46 days so that would have serious consequences to our health! In Daniel 10:3 we read about a partial fast, where Daniel gave up meat, wine and delicacies, and this is the kind of fast we tend to choose for Lent where we give up something that we love for God. We should choose something that costs us as a reminder that Jesus sacrificed everything for us. This isn't a command from God but a response to the amazing thing he did for us!

Grab a large piece of paper and, as a group, brainstorm things you could give up in these categories:

- Things that mean you would have more time to spend with God e.g. watching TV or going on Facebook/Twitter.
- Things that may have a negative impact on you e.g. magazines or caffeine.
- Things that cost you financially e.g. going to the cinema or downloading music.
- Things that cost you personally e.g. giving up your favourite food or drink.

Just a small sacrifice from us could make a big difference for someone else. How? If your chosen fast saves you money, you could use that to help people living in poverty in your community or across the world. See the **Sacrificial Giving** section (page 18) in this resource for more information.

This quote from Bono (from *U2 by U2*) puts our sacrifice into some perspective in terms of the good it can do:

> *Eight million people die every year for the price of going out with your friends to the movies and buying an ice cream. Literally for about $30 [less than £20] a head per year, you could save 8 million lives. Isn't that extraordinary? Preventable disease – not calamity, not famine, nothing like that. Preventable disease – just for the lack of medicines. That is cheap, that is a bargain.*

'Eight million people die every year for the price of going out to the movies and buying an ice cream.'

More to think about (10 minutes – optional)

Have one of the group read one of the following two translations of
Matthew 6:16–18:

> *When you practice some appetite-denying discipline to better concentrate
> on God, don't make a production out of it. It might turn you into a small-
> time celebrity but it won't make you a saint. If you 'go into training'
> inwardly, act normal outwardly. Shampoo and comb your hair, brush your
> teeth, wash your face. God doesn't require attention-getting devices. He
> won't overlook what you are doing; he'll reward you well.* (The Message)

> *When you fast, do not look sombre as the hypocrites do, for they disfigure
> their faces to show men they are fasting. I tell you the truth, they have
> received their reward in full. But when you fast, put oil on your head and
> wash your face, so that it will not be obvious to men that you are fasting,
> but only to your Father, who is unseen; and your Father, who sees what is
> done in secret, will reward you.* (NIV)

Pick some of the questions below to get a discussion going around fasting:

- The Pharisees liked to fast on market days so there were more
  people around to see them. When you think about fasting from
  something that is important to you, do you want lots of people to
  know about your sacrifice?

- In these verses, is Jesus saying no one must ever know you're
  fasting or is he making a different point?

- When Jesus fasted, the devil tried to tempt him. When you think
  about fasting, what objections raise their heads? How do you feel
  about going without something you normally enjoy?

Pray (10 minutes)

Jesus took 40 days to fast, to focus on God and to prepare himself for his
ministry so that he was ready to give up absolutely everything to follow God's
will, even to the cross. Allow everyone to spread out around the room and spend
5–10 minutes in quiet reflection about Jesus' obedience to God. Challenge them
to think about where they're at with God; whether they are fully surrendered to
him, ways in which they'd like to focus more on him and how they'd like to use
Lent to prepare themselves for the tasks God has for them. This is also a great
time for everyone to pray about what they will give up for Lent.

Jesus took
40 days
to fast, to
focus on
God and
to prepare
himself
for his
ministry.

- You may choose to project images onto a screen that help them focus or centre the activity round a cross.
- You could use the following quote to get people thinking: *'Fasting can bring breakthroughs in the spiritual realm that will never happen in any other way. It is a means of God's grace and blessing that should not be neglected any longer.'* (Richard J. Foster, *Celebration of Discipline.*)
- It may help for everyone to have paper and a pen so they can write things down if they wish.

Act

As part of, or in addition to their fast, ask each member of the group to bring one luxury item to the next session that they think would bless someone else. (In Session 2 you will use these luxuries to make small hampers to go to members of the community who are in need so you might want to think about good quality items like biscuits, drinks, chocolate and toiletries.)

'Life is an exciting business, and most exciting when it is lived for others.'

Activity (10 minutes)

Video each member of your youth group saying what they will give up for Lent, upload the video to YouTube and send us the link (info@soulaction.org) so we can add it to our website!

Take it further

If you'd like to go a bit deeper into this week's topics, you could discuss the following:

- Is there anything you would struggle to give up for God? Why do you think that thing is so important to you?
- Consider these words that Jesus spoke to his disciples: *'If anyone would come after me, he must deny himself and take up his cross and follow me. For whoever wants to save his life will lose it, but whoever loses his life for me will find it. What good will it be for a man if he gains the whole world, yet forfeits his soul?'* (Matthew 16:24–26)
- Consider this quote: *'Life is an exciting business, and most exciting when it is lived for others.'* (Helen Keller)

Session 2: *Give Something Back*

Each man should give what he has decided in his heart to give, not reluctantly or under compulsion, for God loves a cheerful giver.
(2 Corinthians 9:7)

What's it all about?

So we've talked about fasting and we're ready to give something up but how can that really bless others? In this session we'll look at the heart behind fasting, the ways God wants us to look out for the needs of others, some of the promises he makes as we look to follow him and some of the ways we can give something back to our communities.

Icebreaker: Follow the leader (10 minutes)

How would it feel to be led around by someone you do not trust? What feelings would it generate?

- In pairs, one person puts a blindfold on the other and is responsible for leading them around the room.
- Split into two teams, each with a nominated blindfolded person. Each team has to give instructions to their blindfolded person to locate an object before the other team's blindfolded person does.

Think (5 minutes)

In our communities and in our world there are so many people that do not have the same freedom and choices that we have. This Easter, while we've committed to fasting to deepen our relationship with God, we can also choose to use our fast to give something to someone in need. God told Abraham he was blessed in order to be a blessing (Genesis 12:2–3) and the same applies to us. We have been given so much in so many ways and God asks us to share those blessings with others.

'Each man should give what he has decided in his heart to give.'

Activity: What's hot and what's not? (15–20 minutes)

Part 1 – Global

Bring a few copies of national newspapers and split them up between the group. Have everyone tear out articles about people or groups around the world who are in some kind of need (it may be physical, spiritual or emotional). Stick all the articles to a large piece of paper and discuss what stands out to the group. Are there more or less issues than they expected? Which issues particularly impact them and why?

Part 2 – Local

Each person has four small squares of paper. Write two positive and two negative things (issues or needs) about the area that you live in. Stick these on a wall in two groups – the hot and not. Look at what is written on each side. Are there similar themes?

Read

Isaiah 58:1–7

True Fasting

'Shout it aloud, do not hold back. Raise your voice like a trumpet.'

'Shout it aloud, do not hold back.
Raise your voice like a trumpet.
Declare to my people their rebellion
and to the house of Jacob their sins.
For day after day they seek me out;
they seem eager to know my ways,
as if they were a nation that does what is right
and has not forsaken the commands of its God.
They ask me for just decisions
and seem eager for God to come near them.
"Why have we fasted," they say,
"and you have not seen it?
Why have we humbled ourselves,
and you have not noticed?"

'Yet on the day of your fasting, you do as you please
and exploit all your workers.
Your fasting ends in quarrelling and strife,
and in striking each other with wicked fists.
You cannot fast as you do today
and expect your voice to be heard on high.
Is this the kind of fast I have chosen,
only a day for a man to humble himself?

Is it only for bowing one's head like a reed
and for lying on sackcloth and ashes?
Is that what you call a fast,
a day acceptable to the LORD?

'Is not this the kind of fasting I have chosen:
to loose the chains of injustice
and untie the cords of the yoke,
to set the oppressed free
and break every yoke?
Is it not to share your food with the hungry
and to provide the poor wanderer with shelter –
when you see the naked, to clothe him,
and not to turn away from your own flesh and blood?'

In this passage God deals with the complaints his people have been making and makes a complaint of his own.

- From what you've just heard, what would you say was motivating God's people to fast?
- Why does this make God angry?
- What does God really want from his people?
- What does it mean to 'loose the chains of injustice' and 'set the oppressed free'?

You may want to read out this translation of verse 7 from The Message:

What I'm interested in seeing you do is:
sharing your food with the hungry,
inviting the homeless poor into your homes,
putting clothes on the shivering ill-clad,
being available to your own families.

When thinking about the exploitation of workers (v.3) it's worth mentioning that though we might not be directly exploiting workers ourselves, the clothes we wear, the products we buy and the food we put in our mouths may be produced by people across the world who are being exploited.

What does it mean to 'loose the chains of injustice' and 'set the oppressed free'?

Activity: Helpless?

It's always inspiring to see what Christians have done to change the world. *Amazing Grace* is a fantastic film about how William Wilberforce was motivated to end the slave trade by his faith and despite heavy opposition. There are clips and resources available at www.amazinggracemovie.com and you may want to watch the whole film together one week.

How could you individually and as a group bless your community?

Sadly, though William Wilberforce did much to end slavery, some estimate there are still 27 million people enslaved in different ways today (source: Kevin Bales of Free the Slaves). Sonal is one example. She was 10 when she left her family for the promise of work because they couldn't afford to eat. That promise was a lie; she was sold as a slave and forced to work long hours in horrific conditions. Poverty traps millions of people like Sonal around the world so governments from many nations have promised to halve poverty by 2015. Soul Action undertakes campaigns like 'Not For Sale' to call on them to keep that promise. Encourage your group to log on to www.soulaction.org to find the latest anti-slavery campaign and to add their voice to the thousands of others who are saying it's not OK for people like Sonal to be sold as slaves.

Act (5–10 minutes)

Have everyone place their luxury items into small boxes and then explain that the boxes are hampers that will be given to people in the community as a blessing from the youth group. Decide together where you would like the hampers to go based on the needs in your community you've discussed and the goods you've collected. Ask for two representatives from the group to go with you to deliver the gifts in the next week or so. They should be two people who are willing to report back to the group on how the gifts were received.

Look again at the newspaper cuttings and things you wrote from the earlier activities. What could you do during Lent and Easter to make the negative situations better? How could you individually and as a group bless your community?

It would be great to come up with a specific action at the end of the discussion like offering as a group to serve in a soup kitchen for a night. You could also think about creative ways in which your freedom could be a blessing to others. For example:

• Using the money you've saved from giving up an item for Lent to go to a charity or a project in your community.

- Taking the time to help someone who has less freedom e.g. an old person who can't walk to the shops – could you offer to get their shopping for them?
- Doing something you enjoy doing and using it as an opportunity to raise some money e.g. having a sponsored penalty shoot-out or organising a fundraising concert for family and friends.
- Contacting companies whose products you buy and finding out the conditions and wages of the people involved in the production of these. Ask them to start using Fairtrade materials like cocoa and cotton that offer a fair living wage to their suppliers.

Pray (10 minutes)

As we give to God, he never fails to give back to us. Although it might sound like he gave us a huge task in the passages we've been looking at, he also makes some awesome promises to us if we follow his commands:

'Then your light will break forth like the dawn,
and your healing will quickly appear;
then your righteousness will go before you,
and the glory of the LORD will be your rear guard.
Then you will call, and the LORD will answer;
you will cry for help, and he will say: Here am I.
'If you do away with the yoke of oppression,
with the pointing finger and malicious talk,
and if you spend yourselves on behalf of the hungry
and satisfy the needs of the oppressed,
then your light will rise in the darkness,
and your night will become like the noonday.
The LORD will guide you always;
he will satisfy your needs in a sun-scorched land
and will strengthen your frame.
You will be like a well-watered garden,
like a spring whose waters never fail.
Your people will rebuild the ancient ruins
and will raise up the age-old foundations;
you will be called Repairer of Broken Walls,
Restorer of Streets with Dwellings.'
(Isaiah 58:8–12)

'Then your light will break forth like the dawn, and your healing will quickly appear.'

How does God say our lives will look if we choose the kind of fast he wants us to? (You might want to look at how God says we will be righteous, we will be a light in the darkness, he will guide us and our communities will be transformed. It's also worth focusing on the fact that as we serve God he says our healing will come – this is such an encouragement that we don't need to wait until we think we're 'sorted' in God's eyes before we get on with this stuff!)

Let's remember that God's not a slot machine! We don't give to God and serve others so that God gives back to us. Our motivation shouldn't be what we can get from God but our love for him.

Take it further

Consider fundraising for people enslaved by poverty.

If you'd like to go a bit deeper into this week's topics, you could:

- Listen to a talk for young people focusing on modern-day slavery and what we can do about it. Download the talk for free at www.soulaction.org.

- Consider fundraising for people enslaved by poverty.

- Speak up for the oppressed – use SuperBadger on Facebook to find the latest actions or think about visiting your local MP to discuss the issues with them (see www.tearfund.org/mp for more information).

- Discuss which parts of the Isaiah passages we looked at feel the most challenging.

- Discuss this quote from Mother Teresa: *'We think sometimes that poverty is only being hungry, naked and homeless. The poverty of being unwanted, unloved and uncared for is the greatest poverty. We must start in our own homes to remedy this kind of poverty.'*

Session 3: Connect with God

If you read history you will find that the Christians who did most for the present world were precisely those who thought most of the next. It is since Christians have largely ceased to think of the other world that they have become so ineffective in this.
(C.S. Lewis, *Mere Christianity*)

What's it all about?

In this session we will be reflecting on the amazing thing Jesus did for us on the cross that means we are able to enter in to a relationship with God. We will look at how this relationship is open to everyone through the story of the thief on the cross, and use that as a catalyst to think about how we can help connect other people to God.

'The Christians who did most for the present world were precisely those who thought most of the next.'

Icebreaker: In the loop (10 minutes)

Put together a list of sentences/topics to talk about – these can be anything that will get a discussion going amongst your group! They need to be short as they will be whispered and passed around the circle! Split into two groups of no more than ten then nominate one person to be the 'outsider'. This person must stand outside the circle made by the remaining people. The leader hands each group one topic for them to whisper to the person next to them. The outsider must not know what this is and must guess what the group is talking about. You should have a large 'right' and large 'wrong' sign to hold up when the outsider makes their guess. Regardless of their answer you should put up the 'wrong' sign. How do they feel to be out of the loop?

Feedback (5 minutes)

Get the group to share briefly how they have found fasting and putting other ideas into action. Invite the people who gave away the hampers to tell the rest of the group how the gifts were received.

Think (10–15 minutes)

With a loud cry Jesus breathed his last. The curtain of the temple was torn in two from top to bottom. (Mark 15:37–38)

The curtain in the temple separated the Holy Place from the Most Holy Place. It was the 'Holy of Holies' that was only entered once a year by the High Priest and was believed to be where God dwelt. When Jesus gave up his life on the cross, the heavy curtain was torn in two, a sign that through Jesus' sacrifice, God's presence had become available to everyone.

- What does it mean for us that we can live in God's presence?
- Is it something we take for granted or something we are in awe of?
- What would it have been like to be told God's presence was in just one part of the temple and you weren't allowed there?

Through Jesus' sacrifice, God's presence had become available to everyone.

Two other men, both criminals, were also led out with him to be executed. When they came to the place called the Skull, there they crucified him, along with the criminals – one on his right, the other on his left. Jesus said, 'Father, forgive them, for they do not know what they are doing.' . . . One of the criminals who hung there hurled insults at him: 'Aren't you the Christ? Save yourself and us!' But the other criminal rebuked him. 'Don't you fear God,' he said, 'since you are under the same sentence? We are punished justly, for we are getting what our deeds deserve. But this man has done nothing wrong.' Then he said, 'Jesus, remember me when you come into your kingdom.' Jesus answered him, 'I tell you the truth, today you will be with me in paradise.'(Luke 23:32–34,39–43)

The thief on the cross had broken the Law that was given to Moses and was considered a common criminal who deserved to die in a public and painful way. Yet Jesus said he would see him in paradise. Do you think Jesus' words would have surprised people? Why or why not?

Activity: Get it right, get it wrong (10 minutes)

The youth leader chooses five questions where there is a right or wrong answer about a famous or controversial person (e.g. How tall are they? What do they like/dislike? Did they say 'Y'? Did they do 'X'? Split into small groups where each group has a mobile phone. As the question is read out, each group texts their answer to the youth leader or assistant. The first team to text the correct answer wins. Identify how many groups texted the wrong answer. What picture does this build up of this person?

People hanging on a cross would be looked down upon by everyone as the lowest of the low.

- What groups in your area get looked down on? (For example, those in prison, drug addicts, homeless people, people living on benefits, teenage mothers, asylum seekers.)
- What assumptions get made about them? Are they fair judgements?
- Have you ever been looked down on because people made assumptions about you? Have you been judged because of your age, the clothes you wear, for being a Christian?
- Were those judgements fair? How did it make you feel?

Act: God wants us in the loop (10 minutes)

God didn't stay in heaven and tell us in a loud voice that he understood us. He came in the flesh and blood form of Jesus, he went through many of the things we go through and was unjustly killed to reconnect us to God. He gave up everything to meet us where we're at and this is the model we should take for telling others about him. We can't keep it to ourselves, or stay in our churches just hoping someone will come through the door. We must go out in the same flesh and blood way that Jesus did and connect with people in order to connect them to the Father.

Discuss

How does our relationship with God impact our relationships with others? Do we find it easier to tell people about Jesus in our words or in our actions?

Connect with friends who don't know Jesus

Think about how you could connect better with your friends. It could be as simple as asking them about their interests and getting more involved with things they are passionate about; or just focusing on asking them more questions in conversations than you answer!

Think about how you could connect better with your friends.

Youth For Christ have produced materials to help young people in their evangelism by becoming comfortable with their own story, understanding their friends' stories and by connecting people with God's story. You can find out more about the course (called *The Art of Connecting*) and materials available at **www.hopetogether.org.uk**.

Pray: Connect with God (10 minutes)

God is the life-source of who we are and all we do.

As a group spend some time worshipping God. Focus on what Jesus did on the cross and how that has brought you into a close relationship with God. Think about the fact that because of what Jesus did, you are always free to enter into the 'Holy of Holies'. Remember that God is the life-source of who we are and all we do and we need to stay connected to him.

Take it further

If you'd like to go a bit deeper into this week's topics, you could:

- Read Matthew 25:31–46 'The Sheep and the Goats'. How does this change everyone's view of serving the poor? How does it change your attitude when you see every person in need as Jesus?

- Think about an event you could hold as a group that would be a blessing to non-Christian friends. It could be a social event or you could consider one of the evangelism ideas in this resource.

Think about an event you could hold as a group that would be a blessing to non-Christian friends.

Session 4: Bless Others

If you think you are too small to be effective, you have never been in bed with a mosquito.
(Betty Reese)

What's it all about?

In this last session we will be looking at what our words and our actions communicate to those close to us, to our community and to our world. We'll also consider how we can live out the Great Commission Jesus left us with and share the good news with others.

Icebreaker: 'I am not what you think' (5–10 minutes)

Split into small groups to play a game of charades. One person in each group is given a piece of paper with a job/animal/object that they are. Below this is a different job/animal/object that they are to act out. The group needs to guess what the job/animal/object is. The person doing the acting must not let on that they are actually something different to what they are acting.

> 'Preach the gospel at all times. When necessary, use words.'

Think (10 minutes)

Read these two quotes out to the group:

> *Preach the gospel at all times. When necessary, use words.*
> (St Francis of Assisi)

> *It is clearly obscene to proclaim eternal riches in Christ to those who are struggling to survive due to hunger and malnutrition. It is equally inadequate to lift people out of poverty now only for them to experience eternal poverty separated from God.*
> (David Westlake, Tearfund)

Being God's witnesses means making sure our words and our actions tie up.

Choose one or two of these questions to discuss:

- Think about the physical needs in your community – what do you think God thinks about them?

- How do you think Jesus would act if he lived in your town, village or city?

- Think about the spiritual needs in your community – how would Jesus respond?
- How do you think people react if we just tell them about Jesus but leave them in physical need?
- How do you think it impacts people if we meet their physical needs but don't tell them about Jesus?

Activity: Explain why (5–10 minutes)

How do you think it impacts people if we meet their physical needs but don't tell them about Jesus?

Think of something you've done for someone else. When you do something selfless and look after someone else's needs, people often ask why. Get your group into pairs then ask them to take it in turns explaining to each other why they are motivated to do these acts. Get them to think about God's character and what he has given them; encourage them to pick each other up on Christian jargon they use that might not make sense to someone who doesn't know Jesus.

Discuss (5 minutes)

But I tell you the truth: It is for your good that I am going away. Unless I go away, the Counsellor will not come to you; but if I go, I will send him to you. (John 16:7)

But you will receive power when the Holy Spirit comes on you; and you will be my witnesses in Jerusalem, and in all Judea and Samaria, and to the ends of the earth. (Acts 1:8)

Jesus did his work on the cross and then he left us a job to do. He did everything that needed to be done for every person to receive forgiveness and have a relationship with God. The only thing left was to make sure people knew about it and that's what he asks us to do! Thankfully he didn't leave us alone; he gave us the Holy Spirit who gives us the power we need.

- In the verses we just read Jesus says it's better for us to be filled with the Holy Spirit than for him to be around. Why do you think that is?
- How do you feel about telling people about Jesus? Does this excite you or fill you with fear? What is it that makes you nervous?

Activity: Global expressions (15 minutes – 5 on each)

Jesus talked about us being witnesses in Jerusalem, Judea and Samaria and the rest of the world. For us Jerusalem is our home, while Judea and Samaria are our schools/communities. Grab three large pieces of paper and write 'home' on one, 'school/community' on another and 'the world' on another. Then, as a group, brainstorm some ideas you could put into practice over the coming weeks to be a blessing and a witness to those groups. For example:

- **Home:** Offer to the do the washing up for your parents or help a sibling with their chores.
- **School/Community:** Hand out small Easter eggs for free at school or pick up litter in your street. Check out the other mission ideas in this resource!
- **World:** Get involved with charities like Soul Action, Compassion, Tearfund and others who work in some of the world's poorest communities. You could raise money for the charity, use your voice in one of their campaigns to shout against injustice or even think about serving with a project abroad.

Ask each member of the group to commit (either in their heart or to the rest of the group) to one action from each of the three categories that they can do in the next week before you all meet together again. Take some time at the start of your next session to feed back about how things went and what people might do in the following week.

Pray (5 minutes)

Many of us feel daunted when we think about telling others about our faith. Maybe we're worried they will judge us, or perhaps we struggle to find the right words to say. The first disciples were threatened because of the words they spoke but they prayed that God would give them great boldness (Acts 4:29). Together take a few minutes to pray for boldness that you might proclaim Jesus effectively.

> Many of us feel daunted when we think about telling others about our faith.

End the session by getting everyone to close their eyes and remember that we don't do any of these things to earn God's love. The cross shows us that God loves us even though we don't deserve it; he will never love us any more or any less than he already does. He accepts us as we are and forgives us when we get things wrong. We love others and try to take care of them in response to all that God has given us and can only do it in his strength and love. Pray that God will help your reach out to the community around you with his love that they might have the joy of knowing the true meaning of Easter.

Take it further

'Let us not love with words or tongue but with actions and in truth.'

If you'd like to go a bit deeper into this week's topics, you could:

- Download the Actions Speak Louder PowerPoint meditation presentation from www.soulaction.org and play it to your group.

- Reflect and discuss Philippians 2:5–8 and consider in which ways your attitude is like that of Jesus.

- Consider this verse: *'If anyone has material possessions and sees his brother in need but has no pity on him, how can the love of God be in him? Dear children, let us not love with words or tongue but with actions and in truth.'* (1 John 3:17–18)

Where do we go from here?

Serving the poor and standing for justice is a life-long journey and studies like this are just the start! Hopefully these four sessions have helped your youth group focus on God's heart for mission and given you loads of ideas for ways to serve in the future. For more information on Soul Action and for ideas on how your youth group can get involved in living out God's mission visit www.soulaction.org.

Serving the poor and standing for justice is a life-long journey.

What Easter Means to Me »

Nathalie Saunders

(Nathalie is studying for her A levels at Godalming College, Surrey)

My first Easter as a Christian was spent mostly at church. I felt distant from God and I was praying that Easter would give me a chance to draw close again. But despite the amount of time I spent there I didn't really feel part of what was going on. The Easter story still felt like, well, a story.

Then I watched *The Passion of the Christ*. I had seen it before, but this time I was watching it from a Christian perspective and I found my heart really being moved. I had found it hard to capture the emotion and reality when I read the Easter story in the Bible. But when I watched *The Passion*, it gave me something visual and tangible to grasp. It made me realise that Jesus really did suffer, that Jesus felt human emotions just like us. When I then reread parts of Jesus' crucifixion in the Bible and the events leading up to it, I was particularly drawn to one line: *'My soul is overwhelmed with sorrow to the point of death'* (Matthew 26:38). I stopped and reread it again and again. Did I really just read that? Jesus was overwhelmed with sorrow? Doesn't he have it all sorted out, being the Son of God and all?

Despite my initial shock the line made me think: Jesus suffered, more than I have ever suffered. Jesus was God, so God knew what pain was. So how could I feel distant from God when he knew what I was feeling? God knows us, and what we feel, so we can take anything to him. It opened my eyes to the reality of the story, I saw the human feeling and pain that Jesus went through, but I also found the joy from the truth that Jesus is alive! It wasn't just a story any more, it was hope, it was truth and it was all a part of my faith.

Roy Crowne, Executive Director of HOPE

I recently met a 17-year-old lad called Peter, who was struggling with so many things. He was convinced that Christianity was totally irrelevant and that church was for a previous generation. He was shocked to discover that most of the disciples were in their late teens and early twenties. Peter saw Jesus as meek and mild; the disciples saw him as a purpose to live for. Then I began to introduce him to people in church whose lives had been turned around by Jesus. They told him of marriages that had been restored, addictions that had been broken, and the healing that came through giving and receiving forgiveness. Peter began to understand something of the power of the cross and it changed his view of Christianity from historical fact to something that could be experienced today.

Easter has the potential to totally transform any life. Yes it happened two thousand years ago but the reality is the power of Easter is present today and continues to work in your life and in mine. It is a relational experience with a living Christ that can cause the greatest transformation in any human being. Easter is not about making bad people good. It's not about trying to improve someone's lot in life. It's not even about trying to improve situations. It's actually about making dead people live. This is why the power is so dramatic – because it changes everything from death to life.

> **Easter has the potential to totally transform any life.**

Easter means that power is now present in our world. As John said, the same power that raised Jesus from the dead is the same power than can transform any situation. In any painful circumstance we face, God is at work and he is powerful. That power is personal, persuasive and has the potential to realise all you can be. Easter for me means life.

The same power that raised Jesus from the dead is the same power than can transform any situation.

Bishop Wayne Malcolm

As I reflect on the three days that changed the world I feel assured of the ultimate triumph of good over evil. As bloody and barbaric as the cross must have seemed to those who witnessed the crucifixion of Christ, the whole scene was really a triumph of love over hate. It serves as comprehensive proof that God's love is much stronger than our sins and that in the end his love will prevail. This fact should give each of us the assurance of God's total commitment to us in spite of our shortcomings and struggles.

It was also a triumph of God's plan over the schemes of men. King Herod, the Sanhedrin and the Romans all had a plan for Christ. They hoped that his crucifixion would put an end to his influence and that the rumours about him being the Messiah would be fully and finally squashed by a humiliating death. However, God's plan prevailed! Today, Christ is adored by millions of people all over the world. He is worshipped as the Son of God and heralded as the saviour of the world. Quiet clearly God's plan prevailed in spite of a conspiracy involving the most powerful minds in that day. This fact gives me hope that God's plan for me will prevail in spite of any plans to the contrary.

God's love is much stronger than our sins.

Easter is ultimately a triumph of life over death. Death is the king of terrors and is considered by many to represent the end of life. However, Christ triumphed over death by rising from it on the third day. This was not a metaphoric resurrection; it was a real one, with an empty tomb and witnesses. His resurrection has taken away the sting of death by assuring us of a wonderful life hereafter.

The three days that changed the world have given us all hope in the ultimate triumph of good over evil.

His resurrection has taken away the sting of death by assuring us of a wonderful life hereafter.

Andy Hawthorne, The Message Trust

It's been said before but surely it should knock us sideways knowing that the first person in heaven after Jesus died was a common thief who had done absolutely nothing to deserve salvation. He didn't even know how to pray properly, he simply said 'remember me when you come into your kingdom' and for the first time Jesus uttered those amazing words, 'Today you will be with me in paradise.' Hundreds of millions since have heard those words from Jesus as they face eternity, not because they have done anything great with their life but simply because they have understood and accepted the beautiful truth that Jesus died on the cross for them and rose again to conquer sin and death.

Possibly the best bit of my job is working in young offenders institutions and seeing young men just like the guy next to Jesus on the cross understanding and responding to this incredible message of Jesus. It was Paul who said in Galatians 6:14, 'May I never boast except in the cross of our Lord Jesus Christ,' because he was a guy who had managed to grasp the sheer glory of the cross. Before the Damascus road he would have seen it as a cruel instrument of torture and death and would have been convinced that anyone who hung on a cross was utterly cursed and beyond redemption. However, after meeting the risen Jesus, it became not only the source of his salvation but something that was his passion and his focus to spread all over the world. Somehow we've got to get to the place where we realise we just haven't got the job done unless every person in our community has heard the message of the cross and resurrection in language they can understand. We must become a church who understands the implications of the cross, what it means to lay down our lives for our communities and how to daily take up our cross. There's temptation to be proud in many other things but only by truly boasting about the cross and resurrection, and living life in its power, will we get the job done.

Tell us what Easter means to you at www.hopetogether.org.uk, on Twitter at www.twitter.com/hopetogether or on the HOPE Together Facebook page!

Small Group Studies

Free Video Resource to Download!

In addition to the following Easter group studies, we've got a special recording of the Easter story told by the gifted storyteller, Pam Pott, free for you to download on our website **www.hopetogether.org.uk/eastervideo**.

Storytelling has become an exciting part of our culture and Pam Pott is one of the UK's leading Christian storytellers. The story is told in four videos (each between four and five minutes long) which would be ideal for you to play at the start of your small group meeting. Though the studies don't depend on you using the recording, we believe this would be a great addition to your meetings and will help listeners engage in the familiar story in new ways.

Pam has spent many years involved in mission work through Youth With A Mission. In the last few years she has branched out into storytelling and has performed at Spring Harvest, Greenbelt and many churches. This art form has real power and Pam is a very gifted storyteller. We at HOPE are very excited to offer you this additional resource and pray it will help you engage with the story of Easter in a fresh and exciting way.

Head to the HOPE website **www.hopetogether.org.uk/eastervideo** to download the videos for free!

This would be a great addition to your meetings and will help listeners engage in the familiar story in new ways.

Notes for small group leaders

The following materials are designed for use by adult small groups. There are four weeks' worth of studies which can be used whenever works best for you in the run-up to Easter. Each week focuses on a different element of the Easter story, providing background insights and provoking questions to help the group think about Jesus' actions and their own actions within the community.

Each week focuses on a different element of the Easter story.

Items required: For some of the sessions it will be helpful to have paper and pens available for the group to make notes as they wish, and also some larger sheets of paper to gather lists of ideas from the group.

These studies have been provided by Church Army which is committed to sharing faith through words and action across the UK and Ireland. Its focus is on the seven out of ten people who have no meaningful contact with a church at all. Church Army has developed these group resources in support of HOPE. To find out more about Church Army see www.churcharmy.org.uk.

The studies were devised by the writer and broadcaster Peter Graystone. He develops new mission opportunities for Church Army. He is the co-ordinator of the Christian Enquiry Agency www.christianity.org.uk, and the writer of the 'Now a Christian' email scheme www.nowachristian.org.

Seven out of ten people have no meaningful contact with a church at all.

Meeting 1

Purpose

To think about how Jesus' triumphant entry into Jerusalem can challenge Christians to make a visible impact on their community.

WHAT TO DO

Introduction

1. Just for fun (but with a serious point), ask the group to imagine that the building in which their church worships has been struck by lightning. Obviously the minister has gone too far this time! For a few weeks, until everyone is sure they are safe, you can't meet in any of the buildings that the church owns or rents. Your group has been given the task of finding somewhere new to meet.

Firstly, draw up a list of some of the things that will be important in your decision. Should it be a place where the congregation is on show, or where they are very private? Must you have electricity, or can you manage without? Will you need somewhere separate for children, or will you all worship together? Will you need somewhere to have refreshments or to play music? When you have worked out the constraints, start identifying some locations in the neighbourhood.

Then introduce a new complication. All the buildings in the neighbourhood are fully booked for the next few weeks. There is no choice – you have to meet in the open air. Have a discussion about where you would select. And then decide whether this would be a disaster or an opportunity.

> Imagine that your group has been given the task of finding somewhere new to meet.

Bible reading

2. Invite one of the group to read these words to set the scene for the story which you will be reading from the Bible:

> *At the time of Jesus, Jerusalem was governed from afar by a brutal and hated government. A military force stamped out all opposition from the Jewish people. It caused misery, poverty and oppression.*
>
> *The governor whom the Roman authorities had placed in Jerusalem was named Pontius Pilate. He had a sadistic approach to ruling the Jews. He had infuriated them by bringing military standards into Jerusalem. They*

bore the image of the Caesar, a man who claimed to be a god. The Jews found it utterly offensive to have these images near their holiest places. But Pilate had terrorised them by having Jewish pilgrims, who had come to Jerusalem to celebrate the Passover murdered in their own temple.

It was Passover time again, so Jews had thronged to the city. Pilate knew that tensions would be running high at the anniversary of this event. So he left his summer residence, which was by the sea on the West Coast, and made sure he was in Jerusalem.

It was a familiar sight for the Jews. Pilate rode into Jerusalem from the west. He was resplendent on a horse and surrounded by a parade of tight-lipped Roman soldiers.

Shortly afterwards, someone else entered Jerusalem as well. He didn't come from the west, but from the east. He wasn't on a horse, but on something entirely contrasting. And the crowd wasn't silent and fearful, but completely different.

'Blessed is the king who comes in the name of the Lord!'

Then invite someone else to read the story of Jesus' entry into Jerusalem from Luke 19:28–42:

After Jesus had said this, he went on ahead, going up to Jerusalem. As he approached Bethphage and Bethany at the hill called the Mount of Olives, he sent two of his disciples, saying to them, 'Go to the village ahead of you, and as you enter it, you will find a colt tied there, which no one has ever ridden. Untie it and bring it here. If anyone asks you, "Why are you untying it?" tell him "The Lord needs it."'

Those who were sent ahead went and found it just as he had told them. As they were untying the colt, its owners asked them, 'Why are you untying the colt?'

They replied, 'The Lord needs it.'

They brought it to Jesus, threw their cloaks on the colt and put Jesus on it. As he went along, people spread their cloaks on the road.

When he came near the place where the road goes down the Mount of Olives, the whole crowd of disciples began joyfully to praise God in loud voices for all the miracles they had seen:

'Blessed is the king who comes in the name of the Lord!'

'Peace in heaven and glory in the highest!'

Some of the Pharisees in the crowd said to Jesus, 'Teacher, rebuke your disciples!'

'I tell you,' he replied, 'if they keep quiet, the stones will cry out.'

As he approached Jerusalem and saw the city, he wept over it and said, 'If you, even you, had only known on this day what would bring you peace – but now it is hidden from your eyes.'

3. This is one of four versions in the Bible of this open air act of praise for Jesus. They are all slightly different, so the eyewitnesses must have recalled different details when it came to be written down several decades later.

All four versions of the story feature a donkey.

Most of the versions, including this one from Luke's gospel, feature the crowd taking off their cloaks and throwing them under Jesus' feet.

There are no olive branches waved in this version – you find them in Matthew 21:8 and Mark 11:8.

There are no palm leaves in this version – you find them in John 12:13, presumably grabbed from the market.

There are no palm trees in any of the versions. (It is too cold in Jerusalem for palm trees to grow!)

Questions to discuss

4. As a group, talk together about some of these questions:

- What do you think was the significance of a donkey? Look at Zechariah 9:9 to get some ideas.
- What do you think was the significance of the branches being waved? Look at Leviticus 23:9–11 to get some ideas.
- What do you think was the significance of cloaks being laid under Jesus' feet? Look at 2 Kings 9:12–13 to get some ideas.
- What do you think was the significance of palm leaves? Look at Leviticus 23:39–40 to get some ideas.
- What do you think was the significance of Jesus doing the exact opposite of what Pilate did? Look at John 18:36–37 to get some ideas.

What do you think was the significance of cloaks being laid under Jesus' feet?

- What made Jesus so compelling that the crowd worshipped him in this way?

- What can we learn from the fact that this remarkable event did not take place in the temple or a synagogue, but in a very public place?

- What do you think made Jesus weep? Is he still weeping?

You and your church

5. Turn your attention back from Jerusalem to your own neighbourhood.

Where are the places that people in the area naturally gather? The church building may or may not be one. There are surely others.

Everybody should think by themselves for a couple of minutes. Then ask one of the group to make a list of all the suggestions on a big piece of paper. (If they are stuck, suggest a local pub, sports centre, park or school to help them begin to think.)

Where are the places that people in the area naturally gather?

When the list is complete, go through them one at a time asking: 'How much do Christians from this church interact with people at this location? A lot, a little, or not at all?'

Focus on the ones which you designated 'A lot'. What could the Christians do in these places in order to announce the good news of Jesus there? This could be either through the things they do or through the things they say. And it could be either in quiet and unspectacular ways or in eye-catching ways.

Point out that what you are discussing has a direct connection with what the followers of Jesus were doing in a very public way in Jerusalem many years ago.

6. Invite one of the group to read this, which describes what is happening in one town in the UK to make Jesus known:

Shena Woolridge, her colleague Revd Sam Foster, and a team from local churches use the whole town of Scarborough as the backdrop to allow people who have never been near a church to encounter Jesus. But she doesn't want to intrude on people's lives in a negative way. Instead she wants people to think about Jesus with all the joy of a festival.

In the summer there are sacred spaces on the beach, at which anyone is able to light a candle in memory of a loved one, to give thanks to God, or to remember a troubled situation. There is also Healing on the Beach, at which a team of people are available to pray with passers-by about anything that is giving them anxiety.

At Easter, Shena organises open-air Stations of the Cross to quietly tell the story of Jesus' life and death. Last year there was a walk from the castle, high on the hill, to the seafront, in which the witnesses to Jesus' life were encountered. And, on the coldest day of the year, Mediaeval Mayhem in the Scarborough shopping centre told the story of Jesus' birth, with jesters and carols to make the Nativity play vivid.

Shena has also devised a trail which allows tourists or locals to take a walk that discovers all the angels that appear in art in the town, and tells the Bible story behind the picture. The trail and leaflet that people follow is now promoted by the town authorities as part of its Chart Scarborough initiative.

(Shena Woolridge is a Church Army evangelist.)

> **In the summer there are sacred spaces on the beach.**

In what ways does what Shena is doing in Scarborough remind the group of the way Jesus was proclaimed in Jerusalem at the start of the last week of his life?

If something happened in your neighbourhood that allowed Christians to let others know about Jesus, not behind church walls but in a place where people naturally gather, how would you feel? Enthusiastic, anxious, embarrassed, or . . .?

Prayer

7. In a time of prayer, lift to God one at a time the places you have mentioned on your list, and the people who gather there. Pray that they will hear the good news of Jesus, and pray about your own church's part in bringing that about.

Close by saying aloud together the very words that the crowds shouted as Jesus rode into Jerusalem two thousand years ago:

Blessed is the king who comes in the name of the Lord!

Peace in heaven and glory in the highest! Amen.

Meeting 2

Purpose

To think about how Jesus' example of taking the role of a servant can challenge Christians to see themselves as servants to their community.

WHAT TO DO

Introduction

1. This is a list of things that, like it or not, need to be done in many families. Give everyone in the group a copy of the list. Ask them to put the list in order from one to ten. One represents the chore that they hate the most (or would hate the most if they don't currently need to do it). Ten represents the task that they don't much mind, or even get pleasure from. Each member of the group starts by doing this individually.

Are the group members all agreed about the best and worst tasks?

Tasks that need to be done	Order from 1 to 10
Ironing	
Gardening	
Filling in official documents and tax forms	
Cleaning toilets	
Vacuuming and tidying rooms	
DIY repairs and decoration	
Emptying and putting out the bins	
Cooking	
Clearing up the mess that animals leave	
Washing up	

When everyone has filled in their own opinions, invite them to compare what they have written with the person sitting next to them. Any differences?

After about a minute, find out whether there were any surprises. Are the group members all agreed about the best and worst tasks, or do some people enjoy what others loathe?

Bible reading

2. Invite one of the group to read these words to set the scene for the story which you will be reading from the Bible:

In the ancient world, humility was despised as a sign of weakness. There were some chores that were too humiliating for decent people to do. They used slaves to do them, believing that slaves were beneath normal human dignity.

On the night before he died, Jesus shocked his followers by undertaking tasks that a slave would usually do. He made them comfortable for the meal by washing their feet, which would have been muddy from the unpaved streets.

Then invite someone else to read the story of Jesus washing his followers' feet from John 13:4–15:

[Jesus] got up from the meal, took off his outer clothing, and wrapped a towel around his waist. After that, he poured water into a basin and began to wash his disciples' feet, drying them with the towel that was wrapped around him.

He came to Simon Peter, who said to him, 'Lord, are you going to wash my feet?'

Jesus replied, 'You do not realise now what I am doing, but later you will understand.'

'No,' said Peter, 'you shall never wash my feet.'

Jesus answered, 'Unless I wash you, you have no part with me.'

'Then, Lord,' Simon Peter replied, 'not just my feet but my hands and my head as well!'

Jesus answered, 'A person who has had a bath needs only to wash his feet; his whole body is clean. And you are clean, though not every one of you.' For he knew who was going to betray him, and that was why he said not every one was clean.

When he had finished washing their feet, he put on his clothes and returned to his place. 'Do you understand what I have done for you?' he asked them. 'You call me "Teacher" and "Lord", and rightly so, for that is what I am. Now that I, your Lord and Teacher, have washed your feet, you also should wash one another's feet. I have set you an example that you should do as I have done for you.'

> 'Unless I wash you, you have no part with me.'

3. An idea to think about:

If this had taken place in the UK in the twenty-first century, what might Jesus have done to leave his followers equally shocked?

Questions to discuss

4. As a group, talk together about some of these questions:

- What lesson do you think Jesus wanted his disciples to learn from this event? Did they learn it?
- Why do you think Simon Peter questioned what Jesus was doing? And why did he change his mind?
- What does this event tell you about Jesus' attitude to slaves? Has the world learnt the lessons he wanted to teach us?

You and your church

5. Turn your attention back from Jerusalem to your own neighbourhood.

Can you identify things that need to be done nearby, but which don't happen?

Can you identify things that need to be done nearby, but which don't happen – because they are unpleasant, because everyone assumes (rightly or wrongly) that it is someone else's job, or because the task is too big for one person?

Everybody should think by themselves for a couple of minutes, either writing down their individual answers or speaking them out. Then compile all the answers on a large list.

Did anyone write an idea for inside the church, or were they all about the community outside the church? (If they did, what does that reveal?)

What would it mean for Christians to take on the role of a servant in the face of these tasks? What would be the likely impact on the community if these tasks were done?

6. Invite one of the group to read this, which describes what is happening in one town in the UK to serve the neighbourhood:

In Weston, which is an estate of social housing near Southampton, Tim Hyde has begun projects that make a real difference to the quality of the lives of people in the community. The local church and its vicar Revd Richard Burningham realised that people who live on the estate would find it impossibly difficult to come to the church building – the culture is very different and it is hard for them to see how it could possibly be relevant. They decided that if people on the estate couldn't come to where the Christians gather, the Christians would go to them.

There has been a great deal of planning to serve the community so that people who live on the estate know that Christians care about their lives.

- Wasteaway: a project to remove furniture that gets dumped in people's gardens because they don't have the means or money to dispose of it.

- Seedbed: an allotment project which grows fresh produce for needy people on the estate. Local people can work or meet others here. The local GP surgery now refers people who are depressed or lonely to join this as a means to recovery.

- Lighthouse Lunch Club: a project in which members of the church act as chefs, chauffeurs and waitresses so that people who are elderly or lonely have a meal, company and spiritual input.

- Swapshop: a project which provides donated furniture and white goods for those who are in need.

- Renovations: a project for young families who have recently moved into poorly-maintained housing on the estate. A tidy-up and a coat of paint can make a big improvement to a person's enjoyment of life.
(Tim Hyde is a Church Army evangelist.)

> If the people on the estate couldn't come to where the Christians gather, the Christians would go to them.

Does what Tim is doing near Southampton remind the group in any respect of what Jesus did the night before he died?

Has talking about chores at the start of the session given you any thoughts about what it would mean for Christians to serve those in the community whose lives do not come into contact with the church?

Prayer

7. As part of a time of prayer, invite the group to name, in one word or phrase, places in the community that have come to mind but which rarely get mentioned in prayer – eyesores, streets that no one can remember walking down, places that are near the church but where no church members live, sites of controversy, and so on.

At the close of this, keep a time of silence, asking people to become aware of anything God might be asking of them in response to what has been in their minds.

Two prayers from the churches of other countries:

On the Thursday before Easter, some churches in Uganda clean the rubbish from their neighbourhood. They regard this as both a personal spiritual discipline and an act of mission. As they do so they use this prayer, which the group could pray aloud together:

> *May God clean my heart as I clean my town. Amen.*

May God clean my heart as I clean my town.

Some churches in South India have a ritual that reminds them of Jesus' foot-washing. Each member of the congregation touches the shoe of the next person, and then brushes his own forehead with the dust. This prayer is said:

> *O Lord, forgive the sins of your servants. May we banish from our minds all disunion and strife; may our souls be cleaned from all hatred and malice towards others, and may we receive the fellowship of the holy meal in oneness of mind and peace with one another. Amen.*

May we banish from our minds all disunion and strife.

Meeting 3

Purpose

To think about Jesus' agonising choices in the Garden of Gethsemane and consider how they challenge Christians about the choices they make – for themselves and for the Kingdom of God.

WHAT TO DO

Introduction

1. Invite everyone in the group to think about the choices they have made. Some of our choices are trivial, such as what to put in a sandwich. Some of our choices are life-transforming, such as whether to apply for a particular job.

Ask everyone to think by themselves about three good choices they have made – today, this year, and in a lifetime. Everyone has a minute or two to think by themselves and they may want to write them down on a piece of paper.

Everyone should have the chance to share this with the group. They should pick one of the choices, small or large, to tell the rest of the group about.

Go on to discuss this as a group:

What has been the best choice that our church has made during the years I have been part of it?

Ask someone to make a list of all the ideas you have come up with. Write the list big enough for everyone to see, on a big piece of paper.

> **What has been the best choice that our church has made during the years I have been part of it?**

Bible reading

2. Invite one of the group to read these words to set the scene for the story which you will be reading from the Bible:

> *These events took place on the night before Jesus died. They happened in a grove of olive trees called Gethsemane. Gethsemane means 'the olive oil press', which is very appropriate as it speaks to us of Jesus crushed and poured out. It is here that Jesus was faced with a choice – he could escape all the wickedness that the world was about to throw at him. Or he could become its Saviour.*

Then invite someone else to read the story of Jesus in Gethsemane from Matthew 26:36–54:

> *Jesus went with his disciples to a place called Gethsemane, and he said to them, 'Sit here while I go over there and pray.' He took Peter and the two sons of Zebedee along with him, and he began to be sorrowful and troubled. Then he said to them, 'My soul is overwhelmed with sorrow to the point of death. Stay here and keep watch with me.'*

'Sit here while I go over there and pray.'

> *Going a little farther, he fell with his face to the ground and prayed, 'My Father, if it is possible, may this cup be taken from me. Yet not as I will, but as you will.'*
>
> *Then he returned to his disciples and found them sleeping. 'Could you men not keep watch with me for one hour?' he asked Peter. 'Watch and pray so that you will not fall into temptation. The spirit is willing, but the body is weak.'*
>
> *He went away a second time and prayed, 'My Father, if it is not possible for this cup to be taken away unless I drink it, may your will be done.'*
>
> *When he came back, he again found them sleeping, because their eyes were heavy. So he left them and went away once more and prayed the third time saying the same thing.*
>
> *Then he returned to the disciples and said to them, 'Are you still sleeping and resting? Look, the hour is near, and the Son of Man is betrayed into the hands of sinners. Rise, let us go! Here comes my betrayer!'*
>
> *While he was still speaking, Judas, one of the Twelve, arrived. With him was a large crowd armed with swords and clubs, sent from the chief priests and the elders of the people. Now the betrayer had arranged a signal with them: 'The one I kiss is the man; arrest him.' Going at once to Jesus, Judas said, 'Greetings, Rabbi!' and kissed him.*
>
> *Jesus replied, 'Friend, do what you came for.'*
>
> *Then the men stepped forward, seized Jesus and arrested him. With that, one of Jesus' companions reached for his sword, drew it out and struck the servant of the high priest, cutting off his ear.*

'Put your sword back in its place,' Jesus said to him, 'for all who draw the sword will die by the sword. Do you think I cannot call on my Father, and he will at once put at my disposal more than twelve legions of angels? But how then would the Scriptures be fulfilled that say it must happen in this way?'

3. Although the way Matthew tells the story stresses the immensity of the choice that Jesus made in the Garden of Gethsemane, other people in the story are making choices too – and they all impact on what happens. Think and talk about the choices that are being made by:

- Jesus
- Peter, James and John
- Judas
- The chief priests
- Soldiers
- The man with a sword

Questions to discuss

4. As a group, talk together about some of these questions:

- What would have happened if Jesus had simply walked away from the garden, returned to Galilee and set up business as a carpenter?
- Have you ever been tempted to say no to what God wanted you to do? What helped?
- Why do people choose not to be part of a church? Are they choosing against the church or choosing against Jesus? How might it be possible to help them make different choices?

You and your church

5. Turn your attention back from Jerusalem to your own neighbourhood.

As individuals, as a church, and in the group you are meeting with today, there are choices to be made. Like Jesus, every single choice we make involves thinking: am I doing this to benefit myself and the people who are around me, or am I doing it to benefit others in the world who haven't yet discovered the

Have you ever been tempted to say no to what God wanted you to do?

love that God has for them? Obviously, sometimes the choices we make are wonderful because both happen together.

Ask everyone to think by themselves (and possibly to write down): How could I as an individual, my church as a community, and this group make a choice in the future that would benefit those in the world (near or far) who haven't yet discovered the love that God has for them?

After some time thinking about it individually, invite everyone to share any thoughts that have occurred to them. Explain that no one has to share private decisions that they have made about themselves and their family (unless they are burning to do so). The most interesting answers to discuss are ideas that would have an impact on the group.

6. Invite one of the group to read this, which describes the choices that one church has made to put the needs of those who have not yet discovered God's love at the heart of its life:

> *In High Wycombe, Debbie Orriss is a member of a town-centre church that is next door to a huge shopping centre called Eden. Debbie wants those who work and shop in the town to think about the choices they need to make in their lives.*

> *A beautiful Quiet Garden in the church offers a thought-provoking alternative to the hurly burly of the daytime shops. Street Angels, trained to offer help to those visiting the clubs, offer a caring alternative to the chaos of the night-time binge. Prayer stations in the churchyard encourage outsiders eating their lunchtime sandwiches to come in. Barbecues in the grounds offering food to passers-by encourage insiders to go out.*

> *Debbie and the church leaders are seeking ways not only to give people a rich experience of God when they venture into the church building, but also to ease the Christians out of the church to share God's love on its busy doorstep.*
> (Debbie Orriss is a Church Army evangelist.)

A beautiful Quiet Garden in the church offers a thought-provoking alternative to the hurly burly of the daytime shops.

The experience of the church in High Wycombe is full of choices. Because the church building is opposite a vast shopping centre it brings the choices people make in their life into focus. There have also been choices about how best to make the buildings useful to others. And choices about whether to bring people into the church, or to take the Christians out of the building to engage with those outside. Have the choices you have been talking about today inspired you in any way?

Prayer

7. Begin a time of prayer by asking for God's wisdom, direction and blessing on the ideas that you have discussed. Thank God for the ideas you had at the start about the good choices that the church has made in the recent past. Then pray about each idea you have come up with.

Towards the end of your time of prayer, have a silence during which people can think about individuals known to them who do not yet have a faith in Jesus as Lord, asking God to become real to them.

Finish by saying together the words that Jesus spoke in the Garden of Gethsemane:

Father, not as I will, but as you will. Amen.

Thank God for the ideas you had at the start about the good choices that the church has made in the recent past. Then pray about each idea you have come up with.

Meeting 4

Purpose

To think about the resurrection appearances of Jesus, and how they can inspire us to pass on the good news of Jesus in our own communities.

WHAT TO DO

Introduction

1. Invite everyone in the group to answer these questions:

- Who was the very first person who told you about Jesus?
- During the course of your life, who has helped you understand what it means to be a follower of Jesus?
- Which Christian people whom you have known in person does it make you happiest to remember?

Lead into a conversation: Apart from God himself, what proves most helpful in becoming and growing as a Christian – is it people, sermons, books or the Internet?

At the time of today's Bible reading only one of those existed to help men and women encounter Jesus – people!

Bible reading

2. Invite one of the group to read these words to set the scene for the story which you will be reading from the Bible:

The gospels were written while it was still possible to get an accurate version of what had taken place.

For about thirty years after Jesus rose from the dead no one wrote down what had happened. This was because it was usual at the time to pass on vital information like this by talking, not by writing. Of course, the first Christians were not educated people who could read, and they expected that Jesus would return any day, so the need to write it down was not compelling. But then the eyewitnesses started to die, and children were born who needed to discover the truth.

So the gospels were written while it was still possible to get an accurate version of what had taken place. All four gospel writers researched what happened when Jesus rose from the dead, because it was so vital. They must have spoken to different eyewitnesses because all the accounts are slightly different. These are some of the events that Luke recorded.

Then invite someone else to read the story of occasions when Jesus, risen from the dead, appeared to his followers. This is from Luke 24:1–12,36–45,50–53:

On the first day of the week, very early in the morning, the women took the spices they had prepared and went to the tomb. They found the stone rolled away from the tomb, but when they entered, they did not find the body of the Lord Jesus. While they were wondering about this, suddenly two men in clothes that gleamed like lightning stood beside them. In their fright the women bowed down with their faces to the ground, but the men said to them, 'Why do you look for the living among the dead? He is not here; he has risen! Remember how he told you, while he was still with you in Galilee: "The Son of Man must be delivered into the hands of sinful men, be crucified and on the third day be raised again."' Then they remembered his words.

When they came back from the tomb, they told all these things to the Eleven and to all the others. It was Mary Magdalene, Joanna, Mary the mother of James, and the others with them who told this to the apostles. But they did not believe the women, because their words seemed to them like nonsense. Peter, however, got up and ran to the tomb. Bending over, he saw the strips of linen lying by themselves, and he went away, wondering to himself what had happened . . .

Jesus himself stood among them and said to them, 'Peace be with you.'

They were startled and frightened, thinking they saw a ghost. He said to them, 'Why are you troubled, and why do doubts rise in your minds? Look at my hands and my feet. It is I myself! Touch me and see; a ghost does not have flesh and bones, as you see I have.'

When he had said this, he showed them his hands and feet. And while they still did not believe it because of joy and amazement, he asked them, 'Do you have anything here to eat?' They gave him a piece of broiled fish, and he took it and ate it in their presence.

He said to them, 'This is what I told you while I was still with you: Everything must be fulfilled that is written about me in the Law of Moses, the Prophets and the Psalms.'

> 'Why do you look for the living among the dead? He is not here; he has risen!'

Then he opened their minds so they could understand the Scriptures . . . When he had led them out to the vicinity of Bethany, he lifted up his hands and blessed them. While he was blessing them, he left them and was taken up into heaven. Then they worshipped him and returned to Jerusalem with great joy. And they stayed continually at the temple, praising God.

'While he was blessing them, he left them and was taken up into heaven.'

3. This Bible passage describes some of the varied (and sometimes surprising) responses by the first Christians to discovering for the first time that Jesus was alive. By looking through it again, can you work out together:

- Who was frightened?
- Who was full of joy?
- Who thought it was nonsense?
- Who was amazed?
- Who remembered what they had been told?
- Who wondered what had happened?
- Who was startled?
- Who began to make sense of what the Bible says?
- Who worshipped?

Questions to discuss

4. As a group, talk together about some of these questions:

- Of all those reactions to encountering Jesus in a living way, which ones have you felt at some stage in your life? And now?
- Why do you think that the first Christians felt such an urgency about telling people what Jesus had said and done? Do you sense that Christians today have the same urgency? What would it take?
- What words would you use to describe the way you feel about talking to friends, family and colleagues about Jesus? Does it make a difference to your feelings if they are members of a church or have no connection with a church?

You and your church

5. Turn your attention back from Jerusalem to your own neighbourhood.

Give everyone five minutes to think alone and in silence. They should write down on a piece of paper: What would you say if someone who does not go to church asked you why you are a follower of Jesus? How does it improve your life?

Explain how useful it is for every Christian to have in their mind a very short explanation of why they have chosen to follow Jesus. It means that when a friend, family member or colleague asks, you are not flummoxed, and you don't have to say, 'I don't know – ask the church leader,' but have something to say. It must be short and simple, because otherwise people lose interest.

Invite everyone in the group to read to the others what they wrote. In every case be affirming and positive about how hearing what they have written encourages other people that it is as easy to talk about Jesus as it is to talk about any other member of your family.

6. Invite one of the group to read this, which describes how one couple are seeking to tell others that Jesus is alive and has made a difference to their lives:

> *In Starbeck, which is near Harrogate, Paul and Sheelagh Easby have a great love for the people of the town, and long for them to discover that Jesus is alive and can make their lives better.*
>
> *They and the teams who work alongside them run Holiday at Home, a summer evangelism project that gives older people the chance to enjoy activities and company in a Christian setting. They run lunch clubs and men's gatherings. At harvest time they invited local businesses to put a display in the church about what they do. The whole building was then smothered in flowers and opened to the community.*
>
> *However, the main impact of what they do to make Jesus known is just through chat and friendship. They walk through the shopping street talking to passers-by so that they become familiar faces. Each Saturday morning the team sets up chairs and invites anyone who would like someone to pray for them to sit down. They have visited 360 homes to ask people if there is anything they would like them to pray for (about a quarter said yes). They make a point of falling into conversation with people in local cafés. And through it all they are making new friends,*

At harvest time they invited local businesses to put a display in the church about what they do.

finding it becomes natural to chat about their church and their beliefs, and watching people come to faith in Jesus.
(Paul and Sheelagh Easby are Church Army evangelists.)

As a group, share experiences of talking about your faith to those who do not belong to a church. Has it proved difficult, joyful, embarrassing, impossible, enriching, constructive? What can you learn from each others' stories, and from Paul and Sheelagh Easby's experience?

Prayer

What can you learn from each others' stories?

7. Begin your prayers by praising Jesus that he is not merely a great man from history, but a risen and living Saviour.

Invite everyone to mention in prayer the name of one person known to them whom they long should discover all the riches that a relationship with Jesus can bring.

Pray for all the members of the group as they seek to become people who spread the good news about Jesus – publicly, privately; in words, in actions; together, individually.

Close by saying together these words, which come from Isaiah 6:8:

I heard the voice of the Lord saying, 'Whom shall I send? And who will go for us?'

And I said, 'Here am I. Send me!'

'Whom shall I send?
And who will go for us?'
And I said, 'Here am I.
Send me!'

What Easter Means to Me

Most Revd Dr Rowan Williams, Archbishop of Canterbury

Good Friday brings us up sharp against the recognition that something is very wrong with the human heart. The cross on which Jesus died reminds us of the countless places where human beings make other human beings suffer unspeakably – and of the fact that most of us most of the time don't notice, and, even when we do, can't do anything to stop it or make things safe.

But Easter also reminds us that the whole weight of human failure cannot extinguish the creative love of God. Conflict and failure are part of the human condition, but Jesus' death and Resurrection turns that on its head. We share one human story in which we are all caught up in a sad tangle of selfishness and fear and so on. But God has entered that human story; he has lived a life of divine and unconditional love in a human life of flesh and blood.

If we can accept the unwelcome picture of us and our world that Good Friday offers, we are, in the strangest way, set free to hear what Easter says. We can give up the struggle to be innocent and the hope that God will proclaim that we were right and everyone else was wrong. We can simply ask for whatever healing it is we need, whatever grace and hope we need to be free; then we can step towards our neighbour. Easter reveals a God who is ready to give you that grace and to walk with you.

> Easter reveals a God who is ready to give you that grace and to walk with you.

What does Easter mean to you?

You've heard from other Christians how Easter impacts them, now this is a chance for you to think about what it means to you! Use this space to think about how you could explain the story of Easter, how Jesus has changed your life, and how he can impact other people.

_____

_____

_____

_____

_____

_____

_____

_____

_____

_____

_____

_____

_____

Pray that as you undertake the missional activities you've decided on, you'll have opportunities to share what Easter means to you with others who don't yet know Jesus.

Tell us what Easter means to you at www.hopetogether.org.uk, on Twitter at www.twitter.com/hopetogether or on the HOPE Together Facebook page!

Go for it!

We hope this book has given you loads of ideas for how you can bless your community this Easter with the love of Jesus. We'd love to hear what happens so don't forget to log on to our website and keep in touch.

It doesn't stop here!

We want to equip you to build on the work you're doing this Easter, so look out for future resources around:

- Harvest in 2012
- Summer events and Christmas in 2013
- A whole year of mission in 2014!

www.hopetogether.org.uk

HOPE: Do more together, in word and action

Acknowledgements

Roy Crowne
Executive Director: HOPE

Board

Steve Clifford
Evangelical Alliance

Andy Hawthorne
Message

Mike Pilavachi
Soul Survivor

Leadership Team

Yemi Adedeji
Church Mission Society

Matt Bird
Make It Happen

Gavin Calver
Youth for Christ

Rachel Jordan
Church of England

Wayne Malcolm
Christian Life City

Kiera Phyo
Tearfund

Laurence Singlehurst
CellUK

David Westlake
Tearfund

Jane Holloway
World Prayer Centre

Wendy Beech-Ward
Spring Harvest

Rob Cotton
Bible Society/Biblefresh

Ian Bunce
Baptist Union

Colin Hardicre
Company Secretary

Thank you to everyone who has contributed ideas, articles and help to this resource including: Ayo Adedoyin, Tunde Balogun, Paul Bayes, Matt Bird, Daniel Brown, Ian Bunce, Steve Clifford, Lucy Cooper, Roy Crowne, Rachel Gardner, John Glass, Paul Harvey, Andy Hawthorne, Agu Irukwu, Peter Graystone, Rudi Page, David Pott, Pam Pott, Steve Price, Nathalie Saunders, Helen Share, Laurence Singlehurst, Caroline Spelman, Stephen Timms, Simeon Whiting, Dr Rowan Williams and Sheila Wilson.

Thanks to Soul Action for providing the youth group materials and to Church Army for providing the small group materials.

With special thanks to the team at Authentic.

Written and compiled by Liza Hoeksma

Edited by Laurence Singlehurst and Liza Hoeksma

Designed by Mike Thorpe at The Design Chapel

Contact HOPE at:
8A Market Place
Rugby
Warwickshire
CV21 3DU

Tel: 01788 542782

Email:
info@hopetogether.org.uk